The Actor in You

THE ACTOR IN YOU

Sixteen Simple Steps to Understanding the Art of Acting

Robert Benedetti

Allyn and Bacon

Boston • London • Toronto • Sydney • Tokyo • Singapore

Series Editor: Karon Bowers
Series Editorial Assistant: Leila Scott
Marketing Manager: Susan E. Ogar
Editorial Production Service: Ruttle, Shaw & Wetherill, Inc.
Composition Buyer: Linda Cox
Manufacturing Buyer: Dave Repetto
Cover Administrator: Linda Knowles
Electronic Composition: Omegatype Typography, Inc.

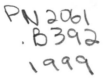

Copyright © 1999 by Allyn & Bacon
A Viacom Company
160 Gould Street
Needham Heights, MA 02494

Internet: www.abacon.com

Library of Congress Cataloging-in-Publication Data

Benedetti, Robert L.
   The actor in you : sixteen simple steps to understanding the art of acting / Robert Benedetti.
      p.   cm.
   Includes index.
   ISBN 0-205-26999-0
   1. Acting.   I. Title.
PN2061.B392   1998
792'.028—dc21   98–19044
                                                     CIP

Printed in the United States of America
10 9 8 7 6 5 4 3 2 1   04 03 02 01 00 99 98

CONTENTS

PREFACE

This book offers sixteen easy steps that lead to an understanding and experience of the acting process. It is designed for students at the introductory level. Although each step provides enough material for one or more class sessions, more than one step may be combined for a single-class session. The instructor should determine the distribution of the work that will best serve the level and needs of the class.

The steps are arranged in three parts. Part I uses examples drawn from everyday life to explain the basic principles of acting for stage or screen. Each concept is put to work in a simple improvisational or game-playing exercise. Part II offers enjoyable exercises to prepare for creative group work in a relaxed and effective way. Part III offers a step-by-step approach to a role. In this part, students will prepare and finally present a simple, short, contemporary scene.

Acknowledgments

My thanks to the many friends and associates who have contributed to my understanding of the acting process, either by their teaching or by their artistry. Special thanks to Lew Palter, Arthur Wagner, Earle Gister, Gil Dennis, Robert S. Breen, John Edwards, Burnett Hobgood, Oscar Brockett, John Houseman, Ted Danson, Patrick Stewart, Joe Morton, Alfre Woodard, Tim Hutton, and Joan Plowright. Thanks also to those who reviewed the manuscript for this book: Rhonnie Washington, San Francisco State University; John Michael Curry, Goucher College; A. Richard Nichols, Penn State University; and Charles J. Richie, Kent State University.

PART I

UNDERSTANDING ACTING

WHY STUDY ACTING?

There are nearly as many reasons to study acting as there are acting students. For some of you, an acting class may seem like an enjoyable way to fulfill an academic credit. Perhaps some of you think it will help you present yourselves more effectively in everyday life. For others, it may seem like a good way to meet interesting people. Some of you may be thinking about a professional acting career. Others may even suspect that acting might satisfy some deep personal need.

Whatever your reasons for studying it, acting can offer great rewards beyond the pleasure of the applause. A psychologist who also teaches acting lists some of the ways in which the study of acting can contribute to personal growth:

> *Finding our inner identity. Changing ourselves. Realizing and integrating our life experience. Seeing life freshly and with insight into others. Becoming aware of the powers of our mind. Risking and commitment. Learning how to concentrate our lives into the present, and the secrets of presence and charisma. Extending our sense of who we are, and achieving liberation from restricted concepts of what a person is.*[1]

In all these ways, the study of acting, even if it does not lead to a professional career, is a meaningful journey of personal discovery and

---

[1]Brian Bates, *The Way of the Actor* (Boston: Shambhala, 1987), p. 7.

expansion. Through acting you can both explore your own thoughts and feelings, have experiences far beyond what your real life offers you, live in new worlds, and say and do things you would never be able to experience otherwise.

What a wonderful thing to do!

Step 1

WHAT DOES AN ACTOR DO?

In the most simple sense, an actor is someone who performs a role in a play, television show, or movie. These three media, and the great variety of material performed in each, make many demands on actors. Few actors are equally good at all. A good television sitcom actor, for instance, may not do well in a dramatic feature film. But there are certain basic things that *all* good actors must do.

First, every good actor creates a performance that is *entertaining*. We can be entertained in many ways: we can enjoy watching a good actor even when this person is making us feel sad, angry, or frightened, because we appreciate the quality of the performance. Paradoxically, watching painful things can be "entertaining" if we learn something valuable from them, as we do from great tragedy. On the other hand, even a show meant to be a pleasant "escape," like a television sitcom, is better if it offers some measure of truthfulness and insight. So we will say that a good actor entertains us by creating a performance that is both *skillful* and *truthful*.

A good actor is also *compelling;* we sometimes say that we "can't take our eyes off" him or her. This doesn't mean that the actor is "showing off" or trying to get our attention in inappropriate ways. What attracts us to some actors are the same things that make us watch star athletes: their effortless skill, their total concentration on the job at hand, their tremendous sense of aliveness. Later in this book we will discuss further what makes an actor compelling in the best sense.

Good actors also create performances that are *believable*. They make us feel that we can recognize their characters as real human beings within the particular worlds of their stories. Notice that believability doesn't always mean "true to everyday life." Not all stories take

3

place in everyday life; they may be set in a historical period, some other culture, or a fantasy world. It is the world of the story that establishes what is "real." Therefore the actor's performance has to be believable within that world.

Finally, it is not enough for an actor to be entertaining, truthful, compelling, and believable. A truly good performance must also *contribute to the particular story being told.* Every character in a story has been created by the writer to fulfill a certain job within the world of that story. Characters are created for many reasons: they may move the plot forward, provide an obstacle to some other character, provide information, represent some value or idea, provide comic relief, and so on. Whatever the character was created to do, the actor must above all create a performance that successfully fulfills that particular job. This constitutes the character's *dramatic function.* Fulfilling the dramatic function of the role is the most important responsibility of a good actor.

To sum up, all good actors strive to fulfill the *dramatic function* of their role in an *entertaining, truthful, compelling,* and *believable* way. That's a lot to ask of the actor, and not even the best actors always achieve all these values in every performance. However, good actors never give up striving for excellence.

Exercise 1.1: Writing a Review

Pick a performance you have seen recently in a film, television show, or play that made a strong impression on you. Write a review of it that examines the qualities discussed thus far. In what ways was the actor's performance *entertaining, compelling, truthful,* and *believable?* How did it serve the *dramatic function* of the character within the story? What were the biggest demands that the role made on the actor? Did it touch you in some personal way?

ACTING IN EVERYDAY LIFE

Actors do things we all do: talk, move, and have thoughts, emotions, and personalities. Even the scripts they perform are usually based on the way people behave in real life and have the same sense of drama that we often experience in sports and other real-life activities. What makes actors special is not *what* they do but the special *way* in which they do it. You already have many of the skills you need to be an actor; what you need to learn are the actor's special ways of using those skills.

Consider the word, *actor.* At its root, it means someone who "acts," who *does* something. Think for a moment: Why do you do things in everyday life?

Usually, you do things to get something you want or *need.* Sometimes what you need is related to physical survival: food, money, or shelter. Sometimes your need is emotional: to be loved, to find peace or beauty. Whatever your need, if it is strong enough, you *do* something about it. You *act* to achieve some objective that you hope will satisfy your need.

Characters in plays, television shows, and movies are shown in situations in which something important is happening. In such highly dramatic situations, whether funny or sad, the needs of the characters are heightened, which compels them to try to satisfy those urgent and immediate needs. This is what makes the story interesting to us; we can feel ourselves in the place of the characters because we also struggle to fulfill our needs every day. Thus we feel *suspense* as we wait to see whether the characters will get what they need, or not. Will the boy and girl get together? Will the villain be stopped? Will the world be saved?

This basic definition of acting will be at the heart of everything in this book: *acting is doing something in the pursuit of an objective in order to fulfill an urgent and immediate need.* Here is a simple exercise which will help you to experience this idea.

Exercise 1.2: Jumps

A. Pick a simple situation and objective related to someone in your group. Choose something that you might really want from this person: to join you on a date, lend you money, work with you on a project, or make an excuse for you for missing class, and so on. Think of your need in a way that makes it important and urgent: you need it badly, and you need it *now.*

When it is your turn, approach them without warning ("jump" them) and try to win your objective. Don't reveal your objective right away, just try to bring it up as you might in real life. If they resist, try different approaches until you find one that works.

Those on the receiving end: Accept what your partners are trying to do, but within the reality of the situation try to make it hard for them. Resist granting the objective as long as possible, but give in when you can't resist anymore.

B.   After you have tried real-life situations, move on to imaginary ones. Pick a situation, character, and objective that you might encounter in life: for example, you are desperate for quick cash and you're going to try to sell this rich-looking fellow your watch for as much as you can get. Again, try various strategies until you find one that works.

   Those on the receiving end: Part of your job is now to find out "who" you are and what is going on. You must accept whatever reality your partner offers and enter it fully.

Keep this exercise simple; it doesn't need to be long, complicated, witty, or emotional. Just let it be as real and natural as possible. Go with whatever comes up and see where it leads you. Afterward, discuss the exercise with the class: What were the most interesting moments? What seemed unreal or unbelievable? This can be an ongoing exercise in your group. As you get the hang of it, some interesting scenes can develop.

Step 2

ACTION IN LIFE
AND IN PERFORMANCE

In Step 1, we said that acting is *doing something in the pursuit of an objective in order to fulfill an urgent and immediate need.* It is this concept of *action* that unlocks your power as an actor. There is often confusion about this term, however, because it has two different meanings.

Critics and scholars use the term *dramatic action* to describe what happens in a play or scene. For example, in Arthur Miller's play, *Death of a Salesman,* the hero, Willy Loman, struggles to prove his worth as a human being by finding success as a salesman. When he fails, he makes the ultimate "sale" by committing suicide in order to leave his life insurance to his family. This is the "main action" of the play. (We call this action "universal" because everyone can relate to Willy's need for self-esteem.) On a smaller level, the action of each scene in the play can be seen as a step in the working out of this main action.

Early in this century, the term *action* began to be used in another way when referring to the acting process. The great Russian director Constantin Stanislavski was dissatisfied with the overblown acting style of his time. Too often, he felt, the actor's display of emotion and technique became an end in itself and overshadowed the meaning of the play. He created a new system of acting aimed at economy, greater psychological truthfulness, and above all respect for the ideas of the play.

He based his system on the idea that everything an actor does in a performance has to be *justified* by the character's internal need. As Stanislavski said:

> *There are no physical actions divorced from some desire, some effort in some direction, some objective.... Everything that happens on the stage has a definite purpose.*[1]

According to this principle, everything the actor does as the character should grow directly out of the needs of the character and should also serve the story being told. The actor cannot "show off" his or her skills for their own sake and is obligated to perform in an economical, purposeful way that serves the meaning of the story.

Stanislavski's ideas have provided the basis for most of the actor training since his time. This book is based on a particular interpretation of those ideas. The central concept is that at each moment of the performance, your character's need makes you do something (your *action*) in an effort to achieve a desired goal (your *objective*).

Some schools of acting use the terms *intention* or *task* instead of *objective,* but they all mean the same thing: *Need causes an action directed toward an objective.* It is this Stanislavskian sense of the word *action* that we will use throughout this book.

Action, then, refers to everything you do as the character to pursue an objective. This includes gestures, movements, facial expressions, and especially *speaking.* In fact, speaking is the most common form of "doing" in performance, and words, at their best, are special kinds of action.

ACTION IN EVERYDAY LIFE

You are already an actor in everyday life. You "act" when you do things to get what you want or need. When your need is important enough, it commands your whole attention. At such times, all your energy and awareness flow through your action toward your objective.

You have seen other people in real life with this kind of total commitment to an action: an athlete executing a difficult play, someone arguing a deeply felt issue, a student studying for a big test, lovers wooing. All these people have one thing in common: *they have a personally significant objective and so they are totally focused on what they are doing.*

---

[1]Constantin Stanislavski, *An Actor's Handbook,* trans. and ed. Elizabeth Reynolds Hapgood (New York: Theatre Arts Books, 1936), p. 8. Copyright © 1936, 1961, 1963 by Elizabeth Reynolds Hapgood.

The more important the objective, the more urgent the action and complete the focus and the more unselfconscious and committed the person becomes.

In acting terms, someone who is doing something with this kind of total commitment is *in action*. Watching someone in action is an invigorating experience. The person seems so "alive" that he or she makes us feel more alive as we watch, even if the action is extremely simple.

For example, I once saw a Canadian mime who began his performance in a striking way: the first spectators to arrive found him sitting alone on the stage, applying his white-face makeup. He worked simply and without the slightest embellishment, but his concentration and involvement were so complete that the spectators quickly became engrossed in watching him. As more spectators arrived, they too fell silent and watched in rapt attention. As the hall gradually filled, the intensity of the experience grew. When at last he finished his makeup, there was a tremendous ovation. The bond with the audience, which his simple but total action had created, was unbreakable for the rest of the evening. Because our energy had joined with his, we felt that we had come to know him.

People reveal a great deal about themselves when they are in action, perhaps more than at any other time. As it is often said, "actions speak louder than words." When people are in action, they are pouring all their energy and awareness into what they are doing and have none left over for deception or self-consciousness. As a result, we judge people who are in action as being *authentic* and *believable.*

Being in action can also help you to conquer the greatest enemy of the actor, self-consciousness. It is self-consciousness that leads to stage fright and awkwardness. When you get your attention off yourself and onto your objective, you naturally become less fearful, more expressive and believable. When you achieve complete focus on an important objective that mobilizes all your energy, your performance becomes *compelling* and you command your audience's full attention.

To sum up: Being in action makes you more *alive, knowable, authentic, believable,* and *compelling.* These are all powerful reasons that being in action, being fully focused on a personally significant objective, is the best condition for you as an actor.

You have been "in action" many times in your life. These experiences can be the basis for developing the same kind of heightened focus on stage. Think back to a time when you were totally "tuned in" to something you were doing, so engrossed in your activity that you became unselfconscious, oblivious of passing time or of outside distractions.

Exercise 2.1: Action in Life

A. For the next few days, notice which people attract your attention: What are they doing? How do they feel about it? What makes them interesting? Notice especially the people in those situations we think of as highly "dramatic": athletes at crucial moments, people in danger, people in the grip of deeply held beliefs, and so on.

B. Think about those times when you have been in action. Select one such time and relive it in your imagination. What made it possible for you to achieve this level of complete commitment and focus?

C. Recreate this episode as a scene for your class.

BELIEVABILITY IN LIFE AND IN PERFORMANCE

Although it is true that we all "act" in everyday life, we do not always act well: sometimes our performance is judged to be "insincere" or "unbelievable." How do we judge believability in real life?

When we are with other people, we send both *conscious* and *unconscious* messages. The conscious messages are what we are trying to communicate, but we also send unconscious signals about our feelings and attitudes. Other people intuitively read these two kinds of information and compare them. When they agree, we are judged to be "sincere" or believable; when they disagree, we are suspected of faking.

For example, if I am trying to convince you that I am extremely interested in what you are saying, but you catch me glancing over your shoulder at the clock, you intuitively compare my conscious behavior with my unconscious signs. Because the two don't agree, you know immediately that I am insincere. Just so, in a stage or screen performance, if you notice behavior from the actor that is inconsistent with the character's thoughts and feelings, you will not believe in the performance.

When we sense a difference between the conscious and unconscious behavior of others, we tend to trust the unconscious behavior, such as body language and telltale qualities of the voice, rather than the conscious behavior. We know that unconscious behavior is likely to be a more reliable indicator of someone's real thoughts and feelings.

This is a matter of special concern for the actor. In life and in performance, you become believable when inconsistencies between your conscious and unconscious behavior disappear and all your bodily energy and mental awareness flows as one. This happens automatically when you are completely committed to your action, when *all* your energy and awareness is focused on your objective and nothing is "left over" to send inconsistent signals. Through action, you can enlist the unconscious aspects of your behavior in the service of your conscious artistic disipline.

Exercise 2.2: A Simple Task

Select a simple physical activity that requires great concentration, such as building a house of cards, counting the floorboards or tiles on the floor, or balancing a stick on your nose. Perform this task in front of your class. Can you allow yourself to become so absorbed in it that you "forget" that you are in front of an audience?

Step 3

INTERNAL AND EXTERNAL ACTION

Action is not just external activity. A cat watching a mouse hole is not moving at all, yet we recognize the drama, the sense of "significant doing" in it. This is because dramatic action is felt even before it has shown itself in external activity; it lives even in the *potential* for doing. At such moments, the action is literally living "inside" us, waiting to erupt into the outside world. So we experience both *internal* and *external* action.

Stanislavski called internal action *spiritual* action, and external action *physical* action:

> *The creation of the physical life is half the work on a role because, like us, a role has two natures, physical and spiritual... a role on the stage, more than action in real life, must bring together the two lives—of external and internal action—in mutual effort to achieve a given purpose.*[1]

For Stanislavski it was the complete integration of internal and external action that produced a truthful stage performance. Accordingly, his acting system was designed to bring about this integration. In the

---

[1]Constantin Stanislavski, *Building a Character,* trans. Elizabeth Reynolds Hapgood (New York: Theatre Arts Books, 1949), pp. 218–36.

beginning, he used psychological techniques which were designed to work from the internal to the external (from the inside out). Later in the development of his method, he began to work from the external toward the internal (from the outside in). As he said, our inner condition is affected by our outer action just as much as our outer action is caused by our inner condition:

> *The spirit cannot but respond to the actions of the body, provided of course that these are genuine, have a purpose ... [In this way] a part acquires inner content [through the development of outer actions.]*[2]

Should the actor work from the inside out, or from the outside in? Throughout the modern period, various techniques have been developed that fall on one side or the other of this question. Some of the modern approaches that work mainly from "the outside in" include that of Bertolt Brecht, who suggested that the actor avoid transformation and instead "demonstrate" the character's behavior for the audience. Polish director Jerzy Grotowski used intensive physical exercises to "eradicate blocks" between impulse and gesture to produce a "holy" actor whose deepest impulses became immediately visible without censorship. Japanese director Tadashi Suzuki also works through intensive physical exercise, featuring the actor's relationship to gravity through extreme forms of walking.

On the other hand, the Stanislavskian tradition tended to stress internals, especially as it was practiced in America. The principal American teachers included Lee Strasberg, who placed great emphasis on emotional and sensory memory; Stella Adler and Sanford Meisner, whose work was character-centered and subtextual; and Uta Hagen who stressed substitutions (which will be defined later).

In general, during the first half of the twentieth century the British acting tradition stressed the importance of externals in the acting process, working "from the outside in," whereas our American tradition stressed the importance of internals, working "from the inside out." Since the fifties, however, most training programs on both sides of the Atlantic have tried to integrate these approaches. The aim is

---

[2]Constantin Stanislavski, *Creating a Role,* trans. Elizabeth Reynolds Hapgood (New York: Theatre Arts Books, 1961), p. 62.

now for a total integration of internals and externals, for both are essential, as Stanislavski pointed out:

> *External action acquires inner meaning and warmth from inner action, while [inner action] finds its expression only in physical terms.*[3]

Each approach has its own vocabulary, techniques, and exercises, and if you work with directors or other actors from one of these schools of thought you will have to devote some attention to developing your own understanding of their approach.

If your action consists only of external movement and speech unconnected to an inner energy, it will seem hollow and lifeless. If your action lives only as inner intensity, without skillful outer expression, it will seem vague and self-indulgent. The most useful approach, then, is to avoid thinking of "inner" and "outer" action as being in any way separate. *Imagine instead a single flow of action that has both an inner phase and an outer phase.* Something happens to which you respond, causing your aroused inner energy to flow outward and to become external action. When this happens naturally, you experience the inner and outer aspects of the flow as a single state. Here is an exercise to experience that flow.

Exercise 3.1: Impulse Circle

A. With your entire group, sit in a large circle, in chairs or on the floor, about eighteen inches apart. Make the circle perfectly round. All group members put their left hands out palm up, then rest their right hands lightly on top of the left hands of those to their right.

   The leader will now start a small, clean slap with his or her right hand. The slap is passed on from person to person around the circle. Once the slap is moving well, try the following experiments:

   1. Focus your awareness on the slap as it moves around the circle. Begin to experience it as having *a life of its own*. Notice how it changes.

   2. Now allow the slap to move as quickly as it can. See what happens when you "get out of its way." Do not *force* it to

---

[3]Constantin Stanislavski, *An Actor's Handbook*, trans. and ed. Elizabeth Reynolds Hapgood (New York: Theatre Arts Books, 1936), p. 9.

go faster, simply relax and react to it as instantaneously as possible.

3. Now let it slow down. See how slowly it can go without dying. Keep the external slap sharp and quick, but slow down the inner impulse as it travels within each of you.

B. Drop your hands, and discuss the many ways in which this exercise is like a scene in performance. Consider these questions:

1. What made it possible for the slap to flow around the group? How is this similar to the way a scene should flow in performance?

2. As you experienced the slap as having a life of its own, how did the nature of the flow change? Did your own experience of it change?

3. Did allowing it to be the focus of your awareness reduce your self-consciousness?

4. How much of the time was it "invisible" as a purely internal action?

5. What was different about the experience when it was moving slowly? What did you need to do to support its life, even while it was passing through the others in the circle?

6. What are some of the ways in which the scene can "die"? What are some of the ways in which we can fail to "pass it on"? How do actors make similar mistakes in performance?

(Repeat this exercise on subsequent days for a good group warm-up.)

In this exercise you experienced how energy flows between people, taking both external and internal forms. It is external when someone is saying or doing something, but more of the time it is internal as every participant receives the energy from others, reacts to it, and then passes it on through responsive action.

In the same way, a scene in a play or screenplay depends on energy flowing from character to character as each one acts and reacts to the other. This chain of action and reaction is a give-and-take, as it moves the scene forward and eventually creates the unfolding of the entire story. Therefore we often say that *acting is reacting.*

TRANSACTIONS

In the Impulse Circle exercise, the slap traveled through the group, each person receiving and in turn passing on the energy so that it could take on a life of its own. You learned from this exercise that it is the chain of action and reaction between the characters that moves a scene. It follows, then, that you and your partners must be good at receiving and sending energy, whatever form it may take—words, gestures, glances, silences, and so on.

When energy is passed from one person to another, we call it a *transaction*. Each transaction is a link in the chain that moves the entire story. Actors work hard to build each transaction in a scene, to make each of them real, and to make sure each moves toward the ultimate destination of the scene. A chain, as we all know, is only as strong as its weakest link.

Remember also how the slap took on a life of its own and began to flow smoothly. When energy is flowing smoothly, the transactions from actor to actor become a continuous process of receiving and sending, leading and following, in which all the actors are both senders and receivers, leaders and followers simultaneously. The following exercises will give you the experience of this simultaneous leading and following.

Exercise 3.2: Leading and Following

A. *Blind leading.* You and your partner lightly interlace fingertips up to the first joint. Your partner closes his or her eyes, and you silently lead him or her around the room. As you gain confidence and control, begin to move faster and extend the range of your travels. Soon you can run! If your situation permits, you can even take a trip to some distant destination. Reverse roles and repeat for the trip back.

B. *Sound leading.* Begin as above, but when you are well under way, break physical contact and begin to lead your partners by repeating a single word which they follow by sound alone. Again, extend your range and speed. Run! *Caution: Be prepared to grab your partner to prevent a collision!*

Review the experience of this exercise. As a follower, did you trust your partner enough to truly commit your weight to your movement?

As leader, did you receive your partner's energy and respond to his or her momentum?

Let's continue with another exercise to explore simultaneous leading and following.

Exercise 3.3. Mirrors

A. You and a partner decide who is "A" and who is "B." Stand facing each other. "A" makes slow "underwater" movements that "B" can mirror completely. Try to keep the partnership moving in unison. The movements flow in a continually changing stream; avoid repeated patterns. Bigger, more continuous movements are easier to follow.

B. At a signal, the roles are instantly reversed *without a break in the action*. "B" is now the leader, "A" is the follower. Continue moving from the deep centers of your bodies; feel yourselves beginning to share a common center through your shared movement; that it comes a common breathing and a common sound which arises naturally from your movement.

C. The roles are reversed a few more times; each time the leadership role changes, but the movement and sound continue without interruption.

D. Finally, there is no leader. Neither "A" nor "B" leads, but you continue to move and sound together.

Watch other partnerships doing this exercise: Do you see how intense and connected to each other they seem? Our listening and seeing of each other in performance should always have this kind of intensity; you will be leading and following each other during a scene just as much as you did in these exercises.

Step 4

UNDERSTANDING EMOTION AND CHARACTER

We've said that the process of acting is basically the pursuit of an objective in order to satisfy a need. But what about the other things we see actors do, especially the emotions they express and the sense of character they project? As you continue in your study of acting, you will discover that *emotion and character develop naturally and automatically from the experience of action as we have defined it.* Let's look at each.

EMOTION

Too often, actors think that they must *feel* something before they *do* anything. You sometimes hear them say, "I don't feel it yet." Of course you want to find the emotional state of your character so that your actions will have the proper quality and tone, but finding the right emotion is a *process* that takes some time. The emotion is the *result* of the process, not its starting point.

You begin work not with the emotion but with the material you get from the script—the words your character says and the actions your character commits—and you proceed from the action to discover the emotional life that drives that action. In other words, you don't create an emotion and then do things because of that emotion: rather, you *do* things in order to fulfill a need and emotion naturally results from that doing.

For example, in real life, your emotions spring from your efforts to get what you want. Think of something you want desperately: if you get it, you are *happy*, if you don't, you are *sad*. If you don't get what you want and it is not your fault, you feel *angry*. When you don't get what you want and you don't know why, you feel *afraid*. When you don't know what you want, you feel *helpless*. In all these cases, you acted on your need first, and so it should be in performance. Remember: *Action produces emotion, not the other way around.*

Even if a script gives you an indication of your character's emotional condition in a scene, you will not "play" that emotion, rather you will "find" it by experiencing the character's action while pursuing the objective. Trying to invent the emotion first is an unreliable and exhausting method that denies the way in which emotion functions in real life.

CHARACTER AND THE *MAGIC IF*

In the same way that emotion arises from action, character emerges from action as well. This is how it happens in real life too, where we call character "personality." Think about how your own personality has developed over the years and how often you "create a character" in real life.

You play a role every time you enter a social situation. In various circumstances and relationships, you pursue your needs by behaving in certain ways, doing and saying certain things in certain ways to other people, and reacting to the things they do and say to you. It is this interaction with your world, this give-and-take of acting and re-acting, this adjustment of your behavior to fit your circumstances and those with whom you interact, that shapes and expresses your personality, your character, in everyday life. It is an ongoing process: as your circumstances, needs, and relationships change, they cause changes in you as a person.

In fact, you play several roles every day—student, son or daughter, friend, employee—each with its own appropriate behavior, speech, thought, and feelings; your own little cast of characters!

This fact was noticed many years ago by the psychologist William James, who said that our personalities are actually composed of many social roles. He called these roles our various *me's*. Behind the "me's," of course, there is one consciousness, which he called our *I*. But our "I" is not rigid and is expressed through all of our "me's," even though some of them may be quite different from one another.

We may even experience situations in which two or more of our "me's" come into conflict with one another. If you are busy being "buddy" with your friends, or "lover" with that special other, the arrival of parents or a boss may cause an uncomfortable conflict between your role as "buddy" or "lover" and your role as "child" or "employee."

Exercise 4.1: Role-Playing in Life

Think about your own experience over the past few days. What roles did you play? How did your situation influence your behavior and feelings? Were there times when you had to switch roles rapidly or when your roles came into conflict?

As you think about how you play various roles in your life, you will also notice that your sense of "I" tends to flow into whichever "me" you are being at the moment. Some of your "me's" may be more—or less—comfortable than others, but they are all versions of yourself. If you are in a circumstance that forces you to behave in a certain way, and you allow yourself to remain in that situation for a time, you start to become the kind of person appropriate to that situation.

When you perform as an actor on stage or screen, you will still have your "I," but you will learn to let it flow into the new "me" of each role you play, even when that "me" is quite different from your everyday self. The qualities of each new "me" have been determined by the writer, who has also created a new set of circumstances, a new world, in which the new "me" lives. One of your most important skills as an actor will be *to allow your "I" to flow fully and freely into the new "me" of the role and its world.* You do this not to "be yourself" but to develop a new version of yourself, perhaps quite different from your everyday self, that is nevertheless "natural" to you, truthful to the character and the character's world as created by the writer, and appropriate to the artistic purpose for which the role was created.

Stanislavski called this process the *magic if. If* you live in the world of the character, and *if* you need what the character needs, and *if* you do the things the character does to try to satisfy those needs, you naturally, "magically," start to modify your thought, feelings, behavior, and even your body and voice toward that new version of yourself which will be your special way of playing the role.

This ability to become a fictitious character, to completely believe in the *magic if* and enter a make-believe world and character, is something we all had naturally as children. It is this childlike ability for make-believe that we need to rediscover as actors, however much we empower it through our adult sense of purpose and technique.

Exercise 4.2: Character in Life

For the next few days, observe your own behavior toward those around you. Notice the way you present yourself differently in various circumstances.

1. Notice changes in your physical behavior.
2. Notice changes in your voice, manner of speaking, and choice of words.
3. Notice your choice of clothing and the "props" you use.
4. Notice changes in the way you think and feel.
5. Most of all, notice how you naturally tend to "become" each of the roles you are playing.

THE ACTOR IN YOU

You now understand that when an actor creates a character the process is similar to what you do every day in real life. In this sense, you are already an actor, and you already have many of the skills you will need to perform on stage or screen. A sociologist noticed this fifty years ago when he said:

> *It does take deep skill, long training, and psychological capacity to become a good stage actor. But ... almost anyone can quickly learn a script well enough to give a charitable audience some sense of realness.... Scripts even in the hands of unpracticed players can come to life because life itself is a dramatically enacted thing.... In short, we all act better than we know how.*[1]

Even though you already "act better than [you] know how," performing for the stage or camera requires that these everyday abilities

---

[1]Erving Goffman, *The Presentation of Self in Everyday Life* (New York: Doubleday, 1959), pp. 71–74. Copyright © by Erving Goffman.

be heightened, purified, and brought within the control of a purposeful discipline. As one acting teacher who is also a psychologist puts it,

> *Almost everything that actors do can be identified with things we do in less dramatic form in everyday life. But in order to express the concentrated truths which are the life-stuff of drama, and to project convincing performances before large audiences, and the piercing eye of the film and television camera, the actor must develop depths of self-knowledge and powers of expression far beyond those with which most of us are familiar.*[2]

This textbook will help you to develop your everyday acting skills into the greater power of artistic technique. Your job is to recognize, focus, and strengthen the natural actor you already are. Only you can do this, but the ideas and exercises in this book provide insights and experiences to help you to fulfill your natural talents.

---

[2]Brian Bates, *The Way of the Actor* (Boston: Shambhala, 1987), p. 7.

Step 5

THE ACTOR'S STATE OF MIND

Stanislavski tells of an acting student who, like many others, suffered from stage fright. He became tense and distracted on stage because he was overly aware of being watched. One day, his teacher gave him the simple task of counting the floorboards on the stage. The student soon became totally engrossed in this task. When he finished, he realized that it was the first time he had been on stage without self-consciousness. Surprisingly to him, the experience was liberating and exhilarating. Stanislavski points out that it was the student's total focus on his task that had truly allowed him to forget about being watched. He was *fully in action,* and therefore became unselfconscious.

From this experience, Stanislavski developed his principle of the "dramatic task," or the *objective.* Instead of counting floorboards, you focus your full awareness on what your character is trying to achieve at any given moment. When you become so engrossed in these objectives that you forget about being watched, you have achieved the condition Stanislavski called *public solitude.*

Public solitude is the ability to experience yourself as though you were in private, even though you are in public. We can see public solitude in real life: an athlete making a play in front of millions of spectators is aware of only the play and may "forget" the spectators entirely. You have seen people driving on the freeways who are so engrossed in their fantasies that they are doing extraordinarily private things even though hundreds of people are driving past them. You yourself at times have been so engrossed in what you were doing that you forgot you were in public.

People who are fully in action are automatically in public solitude. The actor who is totally focused on the character's objective can forget that an audience or a camera is watching. It is at such moments of public solitude that all self-consciousness and fear disappear.

DUAL CONSCIOUSNESS

There is a danger in public solitude, however. Some young actors tend to focus so much on the solitude that they begin to ignore the requirements of being in public. They try to achieve some sort of trancelike state in which they lose artistic control and their sense of performance. Public solitude is not like a trance. Like the athlete, you remain in control, fully aware of your task, and even though you have "forgotten" about the spectators or the camera, they are still in the background of your awareness.

This, then, is the question: Can you be completely engrossed in the action and world of your character and simultaneously be aware of the demands of performance, making the artistic choices required to express your action in a public form worthy of your audience's or the camera's attention?

This question is answered by your capacity for *dual consciousness,* your ability to function on more than one level of awareness at a time. As one of Stanislavski's students put it after a successful performance:

> *I divided myself, as it were, into two personalities. One continued as [the character], the other was an observer [the actor]. Strangely enough this duality not only did not impede, it actually promoted my creative work. It encouraged and lent impetus to it.*[1]

The two levels of awareness, then, are that of the *character* pursuing his or her objective, and that of the *actor* observing and adjusting the performance for the sake of the spectators or the camera.

Different performance situations may require more or less emphasis on one level of awareness or the other. In television sketch comedy, for instance, we may allow a bit more of the actor awareness to be present in the performance. (This is why stand-up comedians are often successful in television sitcoms.) In naturalistic stage plays, on the other hand, we strive to reduce our actor awareness to the minimum.

---

[1]Stanislavski, *An Actor's Handbook,* p. 9.

And for serious dramatic work for the camera, the actor must be completely invisible, leaving only the character. In fact, we say that the camera requires "no acting" at all.

No matter how much you reduce your actor awareness, however, you will never lose it completely, nor do you want to. If you did, you would lose also your ability to make artistic choice.

Dual consciousness may sound difficult, but it is really a very natural ability. When you were a child, a puddle easily became a vast ocean, but it didn't need to stop being a puddle: you hadn't learned yet that something isn't supposed to be two different things at once, and that we aren't supposed to be in two different realities at the same time. As an actor, you will have to forget your adult logic and allow yourself to rediscover this childhood ability to "make believe" in two realities at the same time.

Many actors say that they chose acting as a career specifically because it gives them a chance to use their imaginations in the most complete way possible. Patrick Stewart, best known as Captain Picard on *Star Trek* (and who is also a great Shakespearean actor) says, "What first attracted me to acting was the fantasy world of the theatre into which I could escape from the much less pleasant world of my childhood." Another great actor, Sir Alec Guinness, spoke of acting as a way to escape from "my dreary old life."[2]

Exercise 5.1: Making Believe

Repeat the Simple Task exercise (2.2), but this time give yourself a character and a dramatic situation. If your task was to build a house of cards, perhaps you are a condemned man about to be executed, waiting for the governor to phone with your pardon. See if you can relax and accept the character's reality. Are you able to hold the dual awareness of your character's world and your actor's concerns?

INDICATING

Acting students commonly do too much on stage. They are afraid that it is not enough to simply do what their characters are doing, they also try to embellish, to show us how the characters feel, or what kind

[2]From interviews, used by permission.

of people they are. They posture, exaggerate their emotions, use excessive gestures and facial expressions, and take on a false voice. Their performance is saying something like, "Hey, look at how angry I am," or "Look at what a villain I am."

This excessive behavior is called *indicating*. You are indicating when you are *showing* us something about the character instead of simply *doing* what the character does. Actors indicate for various reasons. Some feel unworthy of the audience's attention and think they have to work hard to earn it; some indicate because they are afraid of losing control over the performance; others simply think it "feels" the way they think acting should feel.

No matter the reason, indicating spoils the performance for the audience. It is part of the fun for the spectators to figure out *for themselves* how the characters feel and what kind of people they are by interpreting their actions. If instead you do this for them by indicating, you have created a performance *about* the character instead of presenting the character itself. The audience may get the message, but they won't enjoy it.

The essence of good acting is to do what the character does, completely and with the precise qualities required but without adding anything superfluous. Your job is to present the truthful evidence of the character's action and leave the judgment and interpretation to the audience.

It is likely that you were guilty of some indicating when you were "making believe" in the previous exercise. You can learn to recognize indicating and learn to avoid it by surrendering fully to your action. When you catch yourself *showing*, get back to *doing*. Repeat the previous exercise with this in mind.

Exercise 5.2: Indicating

Repeat the Making Believe exercise, but this time ask your audience to signal by making some sort of noise whenever they feel that you are indicating. Compare their feedback with your own sense of being in action: Did you know when you were indicating? How strong is your impulse to "show" instead of "do" or to "do too much"?

SUMMARY TO PART I

You now understand the basic concepts involved in acting. We can summarize what we have learned so far.

1. The actor's job is to fulfill the dramatic purpose of the role in a believable, compelling, and truthful way.

2. Acting is being driven by an urgent and immediate *need* to commit an *action* to achieve an *objective* that will fulfill that need. All external actions on stage need to be *justified* by the inner process of need that causes the action.

3. Action naturally produces emotion and character, not the other way around. You start with the *doing* and evolve toward the inner life that justifies it.

4. The *magic if* allows you to let your "I" flow naturally into the new "me" of the created character. *If* you live in the world of the character and *if* you need what the character needs and *if* you do the things the character does to try to satisfy those needs, you naturally start to experience the life of the character and to modify your behavior and thought. This is the same process of give-and-take that develops your personality in real life.

5. Your focus on your objective allows you to become so engrossed in your action that you achieve *public solitude* and lose self-consciousness.

6. Your childlike ability for *dual consciousness* allows your awareness to be simultaneously on your character's objective and on your concerns as an actor.

7. Your job is to *do* what the character does, completely and with the precise qualities required, not to *show* us the character or their feelings by *indicating*.

Having understood these basic principles, you are ready now to prepare yourself to begin work as an actor.

PREPARING YOURSELF TO ACT

THE CREATIVE STATE

You already understand that to be believable, all aspects of an actor's performance must work together consistently with the reality of the character and the character's world. The job requires that all aspects of your self—your body, voice, thoughts, and feelings—be available, integrated, and controllable. These are the tools of your trade!

In the process of "growing up," you may have begun to lose some of the natural playfulness, wholeness, and openness you enjoyed as a child. There may be some aspects of your body and voice, some forms of expression, some feelings, thoughts, and experiences which you no longer permit yourself to use, at least not in public.

In Part II, you will begin to rediscover the ability for fantasy that you enjoyed as a child, when "making believe" was a natural process. You can recapture it best when you are *relaxed, playful,* and *nonjudgmental.* Some psychologists call this *the creative state.* It happens when your internal "parent" allows your inner "child" to come out and play. The first and most important step toward this creative state is *relaxation* leading to openness, responsiveness, and wholeness. The next two steps focus on relaxation techniques and group creation.

Step **6**

TENSION, EFFORT, AND RELAXATION

For most of us, acting arouses anxiety. This can be both pleasurable (as in the quest for creative discovery) and painful (as in the fear of failure). In either case, this anxiety can make your muscles tense and disrupt your breathing and thinking. It also interferes with your ability to react; it "freezes" you and reduces your creativity. For all these reasons, tension is the greatest enemy of the creative state.

When you find yourself scared or stuck, you may attempt to compensate by trying harder, by putting more effort into the work and trying to force your way through it. Unfortunately, this is exactly the wrong thing to do. It only increases your tension and further reduces your freedom of creative response. It is common to see student actors make the mistake of trying too hard; the harder they try, the worse they get. This excessive effort makes them self-aware, obscures their own experience of their work, and reduces their control.

Think of trying to open a desk drawer that is stuck: If you tug at it with all your might, chances are that it will let loose all at once, fly open, and spill the contents. Because you were using excessive force, you failed to feel the exact moment when the drawer loosened; you weren't experiencing the drawer anymore, you were instead experiencing only *your own effort.* Too often, student actors make this same mistake in performance; they stop experiencing the scene and instead become aware of their own excessive effort. This feeling of effort can become their idea of the way it feels to act.

Unfortunately, many actors are driven to excessive effort by their fear of failure or their desire to please their audience. They feel unworthy of the audience's attention unless they do something extraordinary to earn it; the option of doing nothing, of simply allowing themselves to "be there," is terrifying. They feel naked and exposed and become desperate to do something, anything! As a result, they have difficulty experiencing what is really happening on stage.

Here is the secret that will make miracles happen for you as an actor: Acting is mostly a matter of *letting go.* Letting go of too much effort, letting go of chronic physical tension, letting go of a false voice, letting go of your preconceptions about the work, letting go of fear, and, most of all, letting go of who you already are in order to become someone new. The first step in letting go is to stop forcing yourself into unnatural thoughts, feelings, or behaviors.

BEING WHOLE

You know that a believable performance demands total involvement. All the parts of your body, your voice, and your mind need to work together in an integrated way. This integration is a natural state. Even if you have learned habits of movement or voice that made you disintegrated and awkward as you grew up, you can easily rediscover your natural integration and wholeness.

The trick is not *doing* something, rather, it is *not doing* whatever it is that distorts your natural wholeness and responsiveness. Trust that the natural wisdom of your body will take over if you let it.

Exercise 6.1: Playing Cat

Lie on the floor comfortably. Stretch yourself out face up, hands at your sides. Put yourself at rest by yawning and stretching, the way a cat does.

> *To see yawning and stretching at their luxurious best, watch a cat just awakening from a siesta. It arches its back, extends to the utmost legs, feet, and toes, drops its jaw, and all the while balloons itself up with air. Once it has swelled until it occupies*

its very maximum of space, it permits itself slowly to collapse—
and then is ready for new business.[1]

Be a cat. Stretch, arch your back, extend all your limbs to their utmost, drop your jaw, wiggle your arms and hands, and breathe deeply, each time taking in more and more air. When a real yawn comes, encourage it; let the full natural sound of the yawn pour out.

As you rediscover your own relaxed wholeness, you will also realize that you are, by your very nature, connected to your world. Your sense of a separate "I" bounded by your physical body is a limited understanding of your place in nature. Your ideas of an "inner" and an "outer" world are only different attitudes toward experience; the world is one world, which we merely experience as "inner" and "outer." We are in it and it is in us. Your breath itself reveals this, as Mary Caroline Richards points out in her book, *Centering*:

The innerness of the so-called outer world is nowhere so evident as in the life of our body. The air we breathe one moment will be breathed by someone else the next and has been breathed by someone else before. We exist as respiring, pulsating organisms within a sea of life-serving beings. As we become able to hold this more and more steadily in our consciousness, we experience relatedness at an elemental level. We see that it is not a matter of trying to be related, but rather of living consciously into the actuality of being related. As we yield ourselves to the living presence of this relatedness, we find that life begins to possess an ease and a freedom and a naturalness that fill our hearts with joy.[2]

Exercise 6.2: Just Breathing

Take a moment to sit quietly and experience your breath in the manner just described. You are now beginning to experience the

---

[1]Frederick Perls, Ralph Hefferline, and Paul Goodman, *Gestalt Therapy* (New York: Julian Press, 1951), p. 134. (Dell Paperback, 1964.)

[2]Mary Caroline Richards, *Centering* (Wesleyan: Wesleyan University Press, 1964), pp. 38–39. Copyright © by Mary Caroline Richards.

most fundamental requirement of the creative state, *purposeful relaxation.*

RELAXATION

Relaxation for the actor does not mean the ordinary sense of reduced energy or slackness; rather it means that all unnecessary tensions have been removed, the remaining energy has been purposefully focused, and awareness is at a high level.

The kind of relaxation you want is a state in which you are most ready to react, like the cat in front of the mouse hole. Although the cat is completely alert and in total readiness to spring, it is not tense. If it were tense, the tension in its muscles would slow down its reactions and make its movements awkward. The same is true of people.

The best description of the relaxed actor's state is what meditators call *restful alertness.* You are already capable of restful alertness; you don't need to do anything to achieve it, you only need to become still enough to experience it. Do this now, through a simple meditation.

Exercise 6.3: A Meditation

Sit comfortably in your chair, both feet flat on the floor, back and neck straight but not rigid, hands resting on your thighs. Look at a spot on the floor eight feet in front of you or, if you like, close your eyes. Focus your awareness on your breath flowing in and out of your nose. Allow any thoughts that come up to play across your consciousness, then simply return your awareness to your breath. Resist nothing. Sit for as long as you are comfortable. Whatever experience you have is correct.

Your meditation is focused on your breath for a very good reason: breath is life. The word *psychology* means "study of the soul," and the word for soul, *psyche,* originally meant "vital breath." Think about it: when you breathe, you are bringing the outside world into your body, then sending it out again. Your breath constantly reflects your relationship to your world. When you are frightened, you hold your breath because you don't want to let the threatening world in. When you are happy, your breath flows freely. So the way you feel about your world is expressed in the way you breathe it in and breathe it out.

This is why your natural voice, which is based on your breath, is so expressive of your inner state. You can see sobbing, laughing, gasping, sighing, and all the other sounds you make as the natural and automatic reflections of your relationship to your world. This is why actors are careful not to force their voices into unnatural and artificial patterns, and often work hard to free their natural voices from bad habits. Unfortunately, television has turned many of us into "talking heads," causing us to lose touch with the natural breathing which begins deep inside our bodies. Relaxation is the great antidote to all these problems.

The ability to relax can be learned. Psychologists speak of the "relaxation response" which develops with repetition just like any other skill. The following exercise is a classic in the field of relaxation. Although you can quickly learn it on your own, it would be useful for your teacher or a partner to lead at first so you aren't distracted by having to read the instructions. If necessary, a tape recording of these instructions with the necessary pauses would be useful.

Exercise 6.4: Relaxation

Lie in a comfortable position, knees slightly raised. As in your meditation, your breath is the focus of your awareness. Imagine that each inhalation is a warm, energy-filled fluid flowing into your body. Each exhalation carries away with it tension and inhibition, like a refreshing wave. Breathe deeply and easily in a slow, natural, regular rhythm.

Each successive breath will be sent into a different part of the body. As the breath flows into each area, let the muscles there tighten as much as they can; then, as the breath flows out, the muscles release and the breath carries all the tension away with it, leaving the area refreshed and at ease. Exhaling is letting go.

The sequence of breaths will move from the top of the body downward. Increasingly, the regular rhythm of your breathing should make the muscular contractions and relaxations flow smoothly down the body like a slow wave.

1. The *forehead and scalp,* furling the brow, then releasing it; the eyes at rest, closed and turned slightly downward.
2. The *jaw,* clenching, then falling easily downward until the teeth are about one-half inch apart.
3. The *tongue,* extending, then lying easily in the mouth.

4. The *front of the neck,* with the chin extending down to touch the chest, stretching the back of the neck, then rolling the head easily back down.

5. The *back of the neck* with the top of the head rolling under to touch the floor, stretching the front of the neck, then rolling the head slowly down and lengthening the neck.

6. The *upper chest,* swelling outward in all directions so that the shoulders are widened, then easily subsiding, feeling the shoulder blades spread and melt into the floor, wider than before.

7. The *arms and hands,* becoming stiff and straight like steel rods; the hands clenching into fists, then easily uncurling and melting into the floor, uncurling.

8. The *pit of the stomach,* clenching, becoming a small, hard ball, then, with a sigh, releasing.

9. The *knees,* stiffening as the legs straighten, the feet being pushed downward by this action, then releasing the legs and feeling them melt into the floor.

10. The *feet,* with the toes reaching up toward the eyes (but the heels remain on the floor) then releasing and falling into a natural position.

11. The *length of the body,* with the heels and the shoulder blades simultaneously pushing downward into the floor so that the whole body lifts upward in a long arch, then, with a sigh, slowly falling, the body lengthening as it relaxes, melting deep into the floor.

Now take ten deep, slow, regular breaths, and with each breath move more deeply into relaxation, remaining alert and refreshed. The flow of breath is a continuous cycle of energy that is stored comfortably in the body; with each breath, this store of energy is increased. If a yawn comes to you, enjoy it fully; vocalize the exhalation, letting the sound of the yawn pour out.

As you repeat this exercise on successive days, you can give yourself the instructions silently. Keep a steady rhythm that follows the tempo of deep, relaxed breathing. Gradually, the action of the exercise will become natural, and you will no longer need to think of the instructions, giving your full awareness to the flow of contractions and relaxations that follow the breath as it travels down the body like a wave, awakening, refreshing, and relaxing it, making you ready for work. Use this exercise as an easy and quick preparation for all future work. Over a period of time, it will help chronic bundles of tension within your body to break up and dissolve.

As the next and last step in your preparation to begin acting, you will explore the fun of creating with others.

Step 7

CREATING TOGETHER

Actors always work in group situations. In every stage play, television show, or film there are other actors, the director, stage managers, designers, and many kinds of crew members. In any medium, the success of the show depends on the ability of all these artists to work together toward the common goal of bringing the material to life.

When individuals work together as a group, the energy of each individual flows into a common stream, forming one energy that is greater than the sum of its parts. Everyone on the team receives more energy than he or she gives. No member needs to sacrifice individuality; rather, each member finds that his or her individual power is enhanced by having membership in the group.

Such teamwork results from a sense of common purpose and respect. It is achieved when three conditions are met: first, when each member is genuinely *committed* to the common purpose; second, when each member *supports* the others; and third, when all agree to maintain free and open *communication*. Let's examine each of these points.

1. *Commitment.* It is part of your responsibility as an actor to be committed on five levels at once:

    a. To *your own talent,* to acting as well as you can and to continually striving to improve. As the great actor Laurence Olivier said, you must "build on your strengths and aspire to your weaknesses."
    b. To each *role* you play, to finding the truth of the character and of each moment in the performance.

   c. To each *ensemble* of which you are a member, to contributing
      to the success and growth of everyone in it.
   d. To each piece of *material* you perform, to finding and express-
      ing the truth it contains.
   e. To your *audience* and the *world* you serve through your work.
2. *Support for Your Partners.* We all have different reasons for acting,
   but we support each other's objectives, even if we do not share
   them.
3. *Free and Open Communication.* No matter how friendly and sup-
   portive we may be, we are bound to encounter differences of opin-
   ion, conflicting needs, and creative difficulties. All these *problems*
   can become *opportunities* for creativity as long as we can communicate freely about them.

Commitment, support, and *communication* are the cornerstones of teamwork. They are founded on mutual respect and trust. Here are two
enjoyable exercises that explore these qualities.

Exercise 7.1: Falling

   A.   Everybody picks a partner. Stand three feet behind your part-
        ners with one foot back for stability (see Figure 7.1). By
        mutual agreement, your partners start to fall backward keep-

FIGURE 7.1   Falling Exercise

ing their bodies straight but not stiff. You catch them right away, and gently raise them back up.

B. Your partners fall only a short way at first, and then gradually farther and farther until you are catching them about four feet above the floor. If your partners become frightened, encourage and reassure them.

C. Reverse roles and repeat.

Caution: Do not attempt this exercise unless you are confident of being able to catch your partner: otherwise serious injury could result.

Exercise 7.2: Floating

A. Form groups of seven or nine. One person from each group becomes the "floater." The floaters lie flat, close their eyes and fold their arms across their chests. The others kneel beside them, three or four on either side, and prepare to lift them (see Figure 7.2A on page 44).

B. Everyone begins to breathe in unison. When group breathing rhythm is established, *gently and slowly* lift the floaters, keeping them perfectly level. Those being lifted should *feel* as if they are floating.

C. Lift the floaters as high as the group can reach while keeping them level (see Figure 7.2B on page 44).

D. Slowly lower the floaters down, rocking them gently back and forth, like a leaf settling to earth.

E. Repeat with each member of the group.

Exercise 7.3: Cookie Search

A. Everyone in the group chooses a partner. Then the entire group stands together in a clump at the center of the room with eyes closed. Then all spin around a few times until no participants know which way they are facing.

B. Without opening your eyes, move slowly in whatever direction you are facing until you reach a wall or other obstacle. Avoid touching anyone else; feel your way with all of your nonvisual senses.

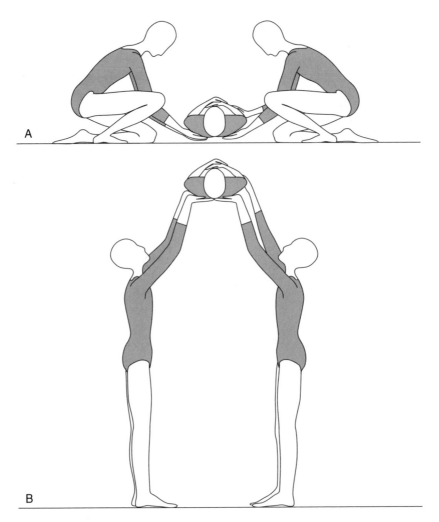

FIGURE 7.2   Floating Exercise

C. When you have gone as far as you can (and still have not opened your eyes), begin to search for your partner using only the word "cookie."

D. When you find each other, open your eyes and wait in silence for all to finish. Enjoy watching the others search. Feel the drama of the exercise.

In this exercise you were not led, but had to find your own way toward the sounds of your partners. Did you feel lonely while searching for your partners and relieved when you found them? Don't be the kind of actors who make partners feel lonely during performance!

Now let's use our collaborative skills to create a group scene.

Exercise 7.4: Tug of War

A. Each member of the group creates—in pantomime—a piece of rope about two feet long.

B. Standing in a single long line, each of you "attaches" your rope to those on either side, so the group creates one long rope.

C. Now separate at the center and slide down the rope until two teams are formed.

D. Have a tug of war. Don't let the rope stretch or break. Continue until one team wins.

This exercise is a good example of performance reality: the rope ceases to be real if any members of the group fail to make their parts real and connected to the whole. This requires that *every individual actor must believe in the whole rope.* That is a good metaphor for the saying, "there are no small parts, only small actors." Our concluding group exercise will illustrate the results of unconditional teamwork.

Exercise 7.5: Group Levitation

A. Stand in one large, perfectly round circle, facing inward. Each of you puts your arms around the waists of the persons on either side (see Figure 7.3).

B. Start to breathe in unison. Bend your knees slightly when exhaling, then lift the person on either side as you breathe in. Do not lift yourself, lift those you are holding, and allow yourself to be lifted by them.

C. As you breathe out, say the word "higher," and try to lift those you are holding higher and higher. Allow the rhythm of the group to accelerate naturally until you all *leave the ground.*

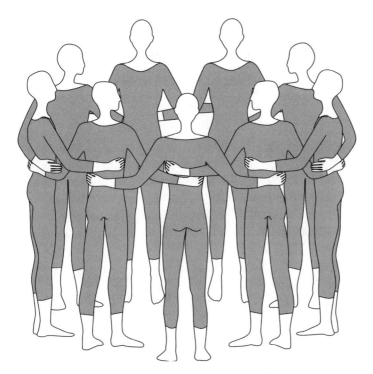

FIGURE 7.3   Group Levitation

Do you see how this exercise symbolizes the way we work to-gether? When the energy of every member of the group is connected to the common goal, the result is greater than the sum of its parts: Everyone gets more energy back than he or she gives!

P A R T III

CREATING A ROLE

THE ACTING PROCESS

You are now ready to approach a role, step by step, in a logical working sequence. You already know quite a bit about this process, but let's map it out in detail.

1. First, you want to understand the basic *dramatic function* of your character within the world of the story, and the *traits* the character has been given by the writer in order to fulfill that function believably.

2. Next, you will put yourself into the character's world and experience his or her *given circumstances* for yourself.

3. In the character's circumstances, you begin to experience the character's *needs* for yourself, perhaps recognizing similar needs from your own life.

4. You then begin to choose the *objectives* the character chooses in hope of satisfying those needs.

5. These objectives motivate you to say and do the things the character says and does—his or her *actions*—in an attempt to achieve those objectives.

6. As you begin to experience your character's world, needs, choices, objectives, and actions, you will find that emotion and a sense of the character's personality will begin to arise naturally and automatically.

This entire process generates a *transformation* in you. Through the *magic if,* you begin to experience the character's thoughts, emotions, and reactions, *as if* you lived in the character's circumstances, *as if* the character's needs were your needs, and *as if* you chose the same objectives and the same actions to pursue those objectives. A new "me," a new version of your "I," forms.

These steps lay the foundation of your work as an actor. Following them will result in a believable, compelling, and truthful performance. Your performance must be the result of this process; there are no shortcuts. As your acting skill develops, you will be able to work more efficiently and effectively, but no amount of posturing, false voice, or trumped-up emotion can substitute for this natural process of transformation and artistic development.

A SCENE OF YOUR OWN

In the remaining steps we will explore each aspect of artistic transformation in greater detail. Step by step, you will apply what you learn to a scene of your own. First, team up with a partner, and together choose a scene that will serve you both well. Your scene may come from a stage play, film, or television script. Since you don't want to burden yourselves with technical problems, like handling difficult language or playing age, keep in mind the following qualities when selecting a scene. A suitable scene will be:

1. *Realistic* and *contemporary,* written in language that is comfortable to you.
2. *Close to you* in age and body type.
3. *Short,* so that it can be read aloud in no more than five minutes.
4. Best of all, a scene which *touches* you personally in some way.

There are many anthologies of plays, films, and TV scripts, and several anthologies of scenes for student actors on the market which may help you. A list of useful plays appears in Appendix B. Whatever the source of your scene, however, it is very important that you *read the entire play or script* from which the scene comes so that your partner and you have all the necessary information about your characters and their function.

SAMPLE SCENES

As we examine the steps in the acting process, I will provide examples of each. Almost all my examples will be taken from two sources, Arthur

Miller's great American play *Death of a Salesman* and a scene from the television show *Cheers*. The *Cheers* scene and a scene from *Death of a Salesman* are presented in Appendix A.

My examples from *Death of a Salesman* will be much more useful to you if you read the entire play as soon as possible. It is available in libraries and bookstores, in paperback, and in many anthologies. Two fine film versions were made of the play: the first in 1951 starring Fredric March, the other in 1985 starring Dustin Hoffman, both available in video. Watching either film will enhance the experience of reading the play *but will not adequately substitute for it.*

Step 8

DRAMATIC FUNCTION

Having read *Death of a Salesman* and the sample scene from *Cheers,* and having selected a scene for your own work, you are now ready to explore each step of the acting process. The very first step is to understand in a basic way the *dramatic function* of the character you are playing.

As the story of a play or movie unfolds, it seems as if the things that happen are caused by the characters. This is not how plays and movies are actually written, however. Usually, the writer starts with the story and its events—the *plot*—and then creates characters who will believably do the things necessary to advance the plot and meaning of the story. Therefore, although it seems as if the characters cause the story to happen, it is actually the needs of the story that determine the traits and actions of the characters.

Actors, then, must remember that their individual characters have been created to do a specific job within the scheme of the story as a whole. This job is the *dramatic function* of the character. Your understanding of your character's dramatic function is crucial to the success of your work. This knowledge will guide you in developing your character and help you in judging the results of your work. As Stanislavski put it, the actor's most important task is *to understand how every moment of the performance and every aspect of characterization contribute to the reason why the play was written.*

Your character serves the story in two ways: by advancing the *plot* through action, and by contributing to the *meaning* through the values expressed in the action. In terms of the *plot,* your character may do things which drive the plot forward, represent a "foil" to frustrate

51

the objectives of another character, or simply provide some information tion essential to the story. In terms of the *meaning* of the story, your character may personify certain values or present a contrast to the values of other characters. This could be in the form of a spokesperson for one of several conflicting points of view or as an embodiment of some quality. Your character may even embody some aspect of the conflict within the main character.

Too often actors approach their characters so personally that they begin to forget the larger purpose for which that character was created. Without a sense of purpose, you may create a character who is alive and believable, but who isn't doing the job it was created to do within the story as a whole. The audience may be impressed by such a performance, but the story will suffer, and you will have failed in your main responsibility.

For example, in *Death of a Salesman,* Willy Loman is a man who, like many of his generation, measures his value as a human being by his success in his work. He *is* what he *does,* and he has no other sense of himself. Such people suffer terribly when they lose their jobs, or even when they retire, because they don't know themselves without their work. Perhaps you know someone who is like this.

In Willy's mind, his success as a salesman depends on whether other people like him. As he grows older and can't compete as well, he is given an inferior position, and is eventually fired. Without his work, he feels not only worthless, but also unliked. He becomes so depressed that he no longer feels worthy even of the love of his family. Eventually, he makes the only "sale" he has left—he kills himself so that his family will collect on his life insurance.

We can say, then, that Willy's dramatic function is to represent the many people who are encouraged by our highly materialistic and competitive society to think that earning money and approval is the only source of self-esteem. These people don't know the difference between *material* and *spiritual* values. Sadly, in our age of corporate downsizing, when entire professions are being made obsolete by technology, we see many people in Willy Loman's situation.

In the sample scene in Appendix A, Willy approaches his boss to try to win back his old territory. This scene shows us how desperate Willy is. He tries every selling trick he knows to persuade Howard. He flatters, cajoles, demands, begs, even offers to take a cut in pay. But Howard has already made up his mind to fire Willy. After this scene, Willy is left with no way to be a successful human being because he cannot value himself without his job; therefore, this scene becomes one of the major steps leading to the climax of the play, Willy's suicide.

As they begin work, both actors involved in this scene need to understand the dramatic function of their characters within the play, and how that function is expressed in this particular scene. They must therefore understand the function *of the scene itself* within the scheme of the story as a whole.

Exercise 8.1: Dramatic Function (First Read-Through)

After reading the entire play or script from which your scene comes, work with your partner to determine the dramatic function of each of your characters within the story, and the function of the scene itself, by answering these questions:

A. If your character were to be eliminated from the story, what would be missing from the plot?
B. How does this scene advance the main plot? What would be missing from the plot if the scene were cut?
C. How would the meaning of the play suffer if your character were cut? Is there some value or point of view expressed by your character? Does your character contribute to an understanding of other characters?
D. What does this scene contribute to the meaning of the story as a whole?
E. With your partner, read the scene aloud to the group. Discuss your understanding of the dramatic functions of your characters and of the scene.

FUNCTIONAL AND LIKENESS TRAITS

In order for your characters to serve their purposes believably within the story, the writer will have provided them with certain traits that make their actions seem "natural." These are called *functional* traits because they permit the characters to believably fulfill their dramatic function.

Willy Loman, for example, is a man who *sells*. Eventually, we realize that he is selling *himself*. He feels that he is worthless until he persuades others of his value, even his own sons. Though Willy has many other traits, it is this deep *insecurity* that allows him to fulfill his main function believably. Whatever else an actor may do in his portrayal of Willy, he must embody this functional trait first and foremost, and let no other trait obscure or contradict it.

Most characters have a host of other traits that do not contribute directly to the character's main dramatic function. These complementary traits "round out" the character, allowing the audience to recognize a real and specific human being who is in some way like us, people we know, or people we know about. These can be called *likeness* traits. Although some likeness traits will have been provided by the writer, this is an area in which the actor is free to contribute personal touches to the role, making it his or her "own."

Arthur Miller tells us, for example, that Willy's wife loves him in spite of "his mercurial nature, his temper, his massive dreams and little cruelties." So, we know he is "mercurial," quick to anger but just as quick to be remorseful. He probably is liked by his male friends, and perhaps was once a bit of a flirt. There are many such "likeness" traits an actor might give Willy, some of which might be surprising or even contradictory with one another—people, after all, are complex. But whatever traits the actor contributes from his own personality and imagination, none of them can be allowed to obscure Willy's functional insecurity.

Exercise 8.2: Functional and Likeness Traits

Examine your characters in the scene again.

A. What traits must they have in order to believably perform their function within the play? For example, do they have to be insecure, ambitious, vengeful, irresponsible, and so on? How has the playwright provided or implied these traits?

B. What additional traits has the playwright provided or implied that help to "round out" your characters as recognizable human beings? For example, do they have a sense of humor, fascinations, quirks, superstitions, and so forth?

C. What traits might you bring to the roles from your own personalities and imaginations that would make them "your own" without obscuring their dramatic functions?

Step 9

THE CHARACTER'S WORLD

Your personality has been shaped partly by your genetic inheritance (your "nature"), and partly by the world in which you grew up (your "nurture"). Every day, you interact with your world. It has physical, psychological, and social aspects which profoundly influence your feelings and thoughts. In reaction to these experiences, your personality is continuing to change and evolve in the direction established by your nature.

A character in a play or film has been given a "nature" by the author. Through it we may even learn something of the character's personal background. The character also lives in a world created by the author (and later augmented by the work of the director and designers). All characters are shaped by their worlds even more than you are shaped by yours, because they and their worlds have been created by the author specifically to serve one another. As an actor, you must work not only on the inner qualities of your character, but also strive to experience the character's world and let your characterization develop within it.

The specific qualities of the character's world are called the *given circumstances*. These "givens" fall into four categories: *who, where, when, and what.* Let's briefly examine each.

WHO

Who refers first to the *personal background* of your character. You learn all you can about a character's personal history from the evidence within the text itself, including the stage directions. You consider the kind of culture and historical period he or she comes from, the social and economic class within that culture, the character's educational background and nature of family life. If this information is not supplied by the text, it may be useful for you to invent some of it for yourself, though you must be careful to do this in a manner that supports and extends the character's function and qualities as determined by the author.

Willy Loman, for example, grew up at the turn of the twentieth century, and was likely the son of immigrants who came to America in pursuit of the "American Dream." Willy was at the peak of his career during the Great Depression, when unemployment was a terrible problem and some men committed suicide because they had lost everything. Given this background, it is easy to understand why the American Dream of "material success through hard work" is the main guiding principle of Willy's life.

Who also refers to the *relationship* between your character and all the other characters who are important to your character, whether those characters are physically present in your scene or not. These relationships have two aspects, the *general* and the *specific*. The general relationship provides basic considerations that make a relationship similar to others of its kind, whereas the specific relationship reveals what is unique to this particular case.

For example, Willie has a *general* relationship to his neighbor Charley. Like many neighbors, they talk about their work and their families, and even give each other advice. But Willy and Charley also have a *specific* relationship that is very important to the overall meaning of the play. Charley is an easygoing man who, unlike Willy, has strong self-esteem. Charley advises Willy to accept himself and his life, and be thankful for all he has. He even offers Willy a job, one which Willy's pride will not allow him to accept. In all, Charley represents a worldview that, if Willy could adopt it, might save his life.

Charley is sharply contrasted by Willy's brother Ben, who lives like a ghost in Willy's mind. Ben is the ultimate embodiment of the American Dream. Like the popular folk hero Horatio Alger, he tells Willy to "go West" and seek his fortune. One of the most important scenes in the play occurs when Willy is playing cards with Charley while at the same time talking to the image of Ben. This scene shows us Willy torn between the two ways of life embodied by Charley and

Ben, neither of which he can really accept because of his deep-seated insecurity. At the end of the play, we see the contrast of Charley and Ben carried on by Willy's sons. Happy declares, "He had a good dream. It's the only dream you can have—to come out number-one man." But Biff says only, "I know who I am, kid."

WHERE

Where the play happens has two main aspects, the *physical* and the *social*. The *physical* environment has a tremendous influence on the action. For example, Shakespeare chose to set a play of great passion, *Othello,* in the hot and humid climate of Cyprus, whereas his play of intrigue and hesitation, *Hamlet,* is properly set in the cold and isolated climate of Denmark. The urban setting of *Death of a Salesman,* where Willy's garden gets only a few hours of sunlight because of the tall buildings that have grown up around them, is a reflection of the in-hospitable and competitive world in which Willy lives.

The *social* environment is also of great importance. In the middle-class society of *Death of a Salesman,* achieving the American Dream, by owning a piece of the earth and paying off a thirty-year mortgage, is a tremendous feat, but it nevertheless is not enough to fill the emp-tiness in Willy's soul because these material things cannot compen-sate for the spiritual qualities that he lacks.

The bar in which *Cheers* is set is very much a character in the show. It is a home-away-from-home, a place "where everybody knows your name." Here the characters share their most intimate feelings and problems, as Diane and Carla do in our sample scene in which social and educational distinctions are unimportant. In this scene, the spunky, street-tough, lower-class Carla is on the same level as her boss, the classy, beautiful but neurotic Diane. Her boyfriend, Ben Lud-low, is an eminent psychotherapist (a friend of Frazier's), and he is attracted to Carla because she is the only one in the bar who *doesn't* treat him with reverence.

In a show such as *Cheers,* the actors, producers, and writers collab-orate to shape characters who will intrigue us for years, with clear-cut identities but who can gradually reveal more about themselves over a long period of time. The producers and writers take care to shape the characters to fit the actors, sometimes even using real-life aspects of the actors (this episode was written because Rhea Perlman, who played Carla, had become pregnant).

As in any good dramatic writing, each of the characters in *Cheers* was developed in relationship to all the others. Diane, for example, is the outsider who is a "fish out of water" in the world of *Cheers,* but she and the denizens of the bar gradually learn to relate to one another despite their great differences. In our sample scene, we see her even giving heartfelt advice to the tough Carla.

The characters in the TV series who appear in only one episode and are played by guest actors, like Ben Ludlow in our sample scene, usually are given virtually no history and limited delineation. We might know only that one is an "eminent psychologist," another a "hockey player," or another "an old girlfriend." It is up to the actor to flesh these characters out. Therefore, guest actors are cast so that they bring some interesting quality to these roles in their very presence before the camera. Being cast in such a role is as much a matter of being in the right place at the right time as it is a matter of acting skill.

WHEN

When a play is happening is important in terms of the *time of day and year. Death of a Salesman* begins in the summer, the season of warmth, growth, and fulfillment, and ends in the fall, the season of cold, decay, and impending death.

The *historical period,* with all its implications of manners, values, and beliefs, is another important aspect of the "When." Although the play is purposely "timeless," *Death of a Salesman* was written in 1949 when the postwar economy was changing and people like Willy were out of place in the technological age that was just beginning. This new age is represented by the wire recorder that stands between Willy and his boss in our sample scene, and which Willy doesn't understand well enough to operate. Today's technology and corporate downsizing have again created many Willy Lomans.

Cheers was set in the present, but the bar had a timeless quality. It was a refuge from the real world, and so the producers were careful to avoid many of the issues and current news events that other shows often used for plot material. Most episodes took place inside the bar, although in later years the characters were seen more and more frequently in the outside world. This change represented a major shift in the tone of the show.

WHAT

Finally, *what* is happening constitutes the most important element of the scene. We should be able to identify the main event of the story, and how the main event of our scene is a link in the chain of events leading to the main event of the story. As you work on a scene, keep in mind the things that have happened before which lead to the scene, and the things that will happen after because of what happens in the scene.

In *Death of a Salesman,* the climax is Willy's suicide; accordingly, the firing of Willy is the main event of our sample scene. Once we have identified the main event in a scene, and understood how it leads toward the climax of the play, we can work much more efficiently to discover the purpose and meaning of each small event within the scene.

For example, in the opening section of our sample scene, Willy has trouble getting Howard's attention because Howard is busy playing with his new wire recorder. We see at once that Howard does not seem concerned with Willy. We will realize later, of course, that Howard has already decided to fire Willy; he probably guesses why Willy is here, and is avoiding the unpleasantness as long as possible by "hiding" in the wire recorder. The actor playing Howard can learn a lot about Howard's character from exploring this cowardly behavior.

In the episode from *Cheers,* the main event is Carla's pregnancy and its effect on her life and her relationship with Ben. There are two parts to our sample scene, the first is with Diane and announces and explains Carla's pregnancy, and the second is with Ben and explains why Carla does not marry him.

In both *Death of a Salesman* and *Cheers,* you can see how good writers shape the events of scenes to fulfill their function within the story. The rule of modern art that *form follows function* applies. When you understand this about a scene, you will see how the actions of your character fit into the shape of the whole. From that understanding of your dramatic function will grow your sense of the inner world of the character's needs, feelings, and thoughts which produce the required actions.

SUMMARY OF THE GIVENS

Here is a list of the givens we have discussed:

1. Who:
   a. The general relationship
   b. The specific relationship
2. Where:
   a. The physical environment
   b. The social environment
3. When:
   a. The time of day and year
   b. The historical period
4. What:
   a. The main event of the play
   b. The main event of the scene and how it connects to the main event of the play

Each of these given circumstances must be evaluated as to its relative importance; don't waste thought and energy on aspects of the character's world that do not contribute to the character's personality or to the action and meaning of the scene.

If the givens of the play are foreign to you, some research will be required. In period plays, the history, architecture, painting, music, and fashion of the time can be very useful. Even contemporary plays may involve circumstances and language which are unfamiliar to you.

When possible, actually experiencing the most important givens can be a great help in rehearsing a scene. Consider working in locations that approximate the conditions of the scene. For example, I have several times held rehearsals for Shakespeare's *A Midsummer Night's Dream* in the woods at night by lantern light, because the "sense memory" of the experience greatly enriches the stage performance.

A note of caution: Beginning actors sometimes try to "indicate" the givens. Indicating is as offensive here as in any other aspect of the performance. Remember: It is not your job to *show* the audience anything about the character's world. Your job is simply to *live* in that world and let it affect you. Trust that the audience will get what they need to understand the scene if you have truly put yourself into the character's world.

Exercise 9.1: The Givens (Second Read-Through)

A. Working with your partner, analyze the given circumstances of your scene and discuss the influence of each on your character and on the action.

B. Rehearse the scene in ways that help you to experience the influence of the givens. You might rehearse in a place which provides similar conditions as the world of the play or impose rules such as *we have to do it within three minutes,* or wear appropriate clothing, and so on.

C. Read your scene for the group. The audience will call foul if they catch you indicating the givens instead of simply experiencing them.

D. Afterward, discuss with the group the influence of the givens on the scene.

Step **10**

THE CHARACTER'S NEEDS

Your character's behavior, like your own behavior in everyday life, is driven by needs. When you feel a need, you are energized—you feel like you have to *do* something, even if you don't know immediately what it is. This arousal can be either positive, as in the anticipation of something pleasurable, or negative, as in the fear of something painful.

As in life, characters may postpone acting on their needs because of either external or internal obstacles. You know from your own experience that the longer an important need is suppressed, the stronger it becomes. This technical trick helps writers to build suspense in a play or film. Shakespeare's Hamlet, for example, spends a great deal of time wondering whether to revenge his father's murder; he finds one excuse after another for not acting on his need. We begin to wonder, how much longer will he wait? What will happen? The tension becomes greater and greater with each passing scene. Finally, in the last scene of the play, circumstance will not permit him to delay any longer, and his action literally explodes.

Hamlet, however, is an unusual character. Most characters, like most people, act on their needs moment by moment in many ways, big and small. Usually, the sequence of events develops like this: Something happens which arouses a need in you. You either react immediately without thinking, or you consider what you might do. You then choose a course of action directed toward some objective that you hope will satisfy your need. In short, *need leads to a choice of action directed toward an objective.*

Let's take an example from our sample scene from *Death of a Salesman.* Remember the immediate circumstances of the scene: Willy has been assigned to territory far from home, and the drive, at Willy's age, is becoming dangerous. His original boss, who was his friend, has died and left his son, Howard, in charge of the business. Willy visits Howard to try to get an assignment in town. As we trace the action of the scene, remember that *need leads to a choice of action directed toward an objective.*

Willy enters and sees Howard playing with his new recorder. Willy needs *his old territory* and at this moment his objective is *to get Howard's attention* so he can ask for it. He tries several times to speak to Howard, but Howard keeps putting him off by playing with the recorder. Willy's experience as a salesman has taught him to "get a foot in the door" by asking about something the client likes, so Willy chooses a course of action, *to express interest in the recorder and use it to turn the conversation to his need.* This goes on for several pages, and forms one *unit of action* or "beat" of the scene. (This is a concept which we will explore in greater detail later; for now, our interest is Willy's need.)

Notice that a need is *internal* (inside you), whereas the objective is *external* ("out there" in the other character). The action you commit in order to try to achieve your objective is a kind of conduit that links the two. Through this channel, your energy, in the form of words and gestures, flows outward. Your need thus drives your action toward your objective, where it collides with the energies of other characters and a set of circumstances. In this way, the scene moves forward.

We come to understand your need through your action. Actors sometimes make the mistake of trying to "play" their need: they try to *show* us how desperate they are, or how lonely, and so on. But as you already know, this results in *indicating,* in showing instead of doing. The writer has constructed your character so that the lines and actions spring naturally from his or her needs; if you have developed your performance so as to be true to the writer's plan, it will be much more satisfying for the audience to figure those needs out for themselves, rather than for you to "show" them what they are.

PERSONALIZING AND THE *MAGIC IF*

You have already learned that a role evolves through transformation: by entering into your character's world, feeling your character's needs, and doing the things your character does to try to satisfy those needs, a new version of yourself—a new "me"—develops called the *character-*

ization. This natural process of transformation, however, will work only if you allow yourself to experience your character's world, needs, and actions with real urgency and significance. As the *magic if* says, you must feel these things *as if they were your own.* This is called *personalization,* and it applies to every step of the acting process.

Many roles will suggest some experiences and behaviors similar to something in your own life, and you will want to use these established connections as a foundation for your personalization of the role. Every role, however, will also require you to reach out into *new* modes of experience and behavior through *observation, empathy,* and *imagination.*

Learn to *observe* interesting human behavior in every way you can—an actor needs a good storehouse of observation. Learn also to put yourself in the shoes of those you observe, especially when they are quite different from yourself. This ability to *empathize* is a very necessary acting skill. Finally, develop your ability to *imagine* what it is like to feel, think, and behave differently. (Surveys have shown that many actors are only or youngest children who grew up depending on a rich fantasy life because they didn't have many playmates.)

Trust that you possess a vast personal potential. If you can engage your own energy in your character's actions within the scripted world, and make that world and those actions real for yourself even if they are unfamiliar, you will find yourself naturally transformed toward a new state of being. In other words, acting is as much *self-expansion* as it is *self-expression.* This expansion, this exploration of new states of being, is the most exciting aspect of the actor's creative process.

EMOTIONAL RECALL AND SUBSTITUTION

If you encounter a character whose needs or circumstances are so unfamiliar that you have difficulty experiencing the role, you might try two techniques designed to help you to connect material from your own life to your work. These techniques are *emotional recall* and *substitution.*

Stanislavski experimented with the idea that the actor could develop a wealth of emotional memories as a resource for the acting process, much as a painter learns to mix colors:

> *The broader your emotion memory, the richer your material for inner creativeness.... Our creative experiences are vivid and full in*

direct proportion to the power, keenness and exactness of our mem-
ory.... Sometimes memories continue to live in us, grow and become
deeper. They even stimulate new processes and either fill out unfin-
ished details or suggest altogether new ones.[1]

There are several techniques by which stored memories may be
recalled. One of the easiest of these techniques is *visualization.* This
involves relaxing deeply and imagining yourself in the character's
world, with all its sights, sounds, smells, the feeling of your clothing,
and so on. Also imagine yourself in your character's situation, with all
the feelings and needs it involves. From these imagined experiences,
you can invite associations from your store of memories. These associations, or *recalls,* automatically become attached to the character's
actions and situation; it is neither necessary nor desirable to "play"
them, simply allow them to "exist."

The key to this technique is *relaxation.* When we relax, the storehouse of memory and subconscious material becomes more accessi-
ble. You may notice that when you do relaxation exercises such as
meditation, memories naturally flood up.

Another technique which may be useful in certain situations
involves making a mental *substitution* of some situation or some person from your own life for the situation or characters in the scene. If,
for example, you are expected to be terribly afraid of another character, it might be useful to recall some frightening person from your
own life and "substitute" that impression in your own mind for that
character. Sometimes your character's situation also may remind you
of a time you felt terribly threatened. Such substitutions will often
arise naturally as you form associations between the world of the
character and your own experience.

Of course, such emotional recalls and substitutions need not be
rooted in real events; fantasy sometimes supplies more powerful material than real life. Your dreams and imagination already provide a
storehouse of situations and characters that are as useful in your acting as anything from your real life.

A word of caution: As useful as emotional recalls and substitutions
may sometimes be, they can also be dangerous. First, memories can
be very powerful, and can *overwhelm artistic control.* Second, recalls
and substitutions can become *obstacles between you and your scene part-*

---

[1]Stanislavski, *An Actor's Handbook,* p. 56.

ners; it is awful to be on stage with someone who is looking at you with that vacant stare because that actor is "seeing" someone else in his or her own mind or is busy reliving the day the family dog died. Third, and most dangerous, the emotional power of recalls may distract you from your focus on your objective and lure you into *playing an emotional state.* For all these reasons, recalls and substitutions may be carefully used in rehearsal but are and absolutely *not* intended for use in performance. Stanislavski himself eventually abandoned the technique.

Exercise 10.1: Personalization (Third Read-Through)

A. Place yourself comfortably at rest and do the relaxation exercise.

B. Now go through your scene mentally; picture the entire circumstance and live through your character's actions as if you were actually doing them in those circumstances. Let your body respond freely. (This technique, used by Olympic athletes with great success, is called *visuo-motor-behavior rehearsal* [VMBR].)

C. As you live through the scene, notice the emotional associations that arise. Do you remember events from your past? Do the other characters remind you of people you have known? Let yourself relive these memories fully.

D. Review this exercise and evaluate any connections that were made. Are they useful to the scene? Do they need to be altered to meet the exact demands of the scene?

E. Rehearse your scene and simply allow these associations to "exist." Avoid indicating them.

F. Again read through your scene in front of the group. After the reading, discuss it with the group. Were you able to endow your character's need, situation, and action with personal significance? Did the character seem more real to the group? Are you beginning to feel a transformation into the character?

By now, you are well on your way to having your scene memorized; subsequent exercises will require that you have your lines thoroughly memorized. We call this getting "off book."

THE CHARACTER'S MIND

You already know that your character serves a dramatic function through a sequence of actions, by doing and saying certain things in certain ways so as to move the story forward and give it the proper meaning. The writer created your character so that these actions are believable and natural to the role. One of the most important parts of your job is to discover the inner process of thought that lies behind these external actions.

A novelist can take you inside a character's mind to explain what the person is thinking, but a dramatist can only *imply* the character's thought through the character's action. You have to examine the action and recreate the mental processes that produces it. This is what Stanislavski called *justifying* the outer action by connecting it to an inner process. This will be the greatest creative and personal contribution you will make to your performance, and it will be the foundation of all the other work you do on the role.

Let's examine the connection between inner and outer action in detail. Remember the Impulse Circle exercise: the slap you received was a stimulus; it *aroused* you and caused a *reaction* as it passed through you, then left you as an *action* as you slapped the next person's hand. Your action then became a stimulus for the next person, generated a reaction, which in turn generated another action, and so the slap moved around the circle. Similarly, a dramatic scene moves as the characters react and act on one another. *Reaction turns into action,* forming the chain of action–reaction–action–reaction, and so on, which moves the story forward.

The Impulse Circle exercise was not exactly like a scene, of course. In the exercise, the slap was more or less the same as it moved around the circle. After a while, that would become repetitious and boring. In a dramatic scene, the energy leaving each character as action is not the same as that which entered as stimulus; it is altered as it passes through each character by his or her needs, personality, and objectives. So in a scene, the "slap" is continually changing as the story evolves, and this makes it more interesting and suspenseful.

From this, you can see that each character is a channel through which the energy of the story flows, and that each character contributes something special to the changing nature of that energy as the story unfolds. The inner thought process of each character is designed to produce the proper effect on the story in each link of the chain of reaction–action. You will examine this inner process in this Step; you will explore *what happens inside you as your reaction to a stimulus turns into an action directed toward an objective.*

Let's begin to examine this psychological aspect of action by setting up a hypothetical situation: Imagine that you see a notice that I am directing a play, and there is a part in this play that you want very badly. Even though you fear my possible rejection, your need is strong enough that you come to see me. You tell me why you are perfect for the part and ask me to cast you; I audition you, and you get the part.

We will breakdown the situation into step-by-step components. First, you saw the notice, which gave you a *stimulus.* This stimulus touched on your *need* to play the part. Although you wanted the part, you were also afraid of my rejection; these feelings connected to the need influenced your *attitude.* However, your need was strong enough to overcome your fear. Therefore, after *considering* your alternatives, you *chose* an *action* directed toward an *objective:* you came to see me and tried to persuade me to cast you.

Our sample situation illustrates the internal process by which action is formed: a *stimulus* arouses a *need* about which you have an *attitude,* which generates a *consideration* of alternatives leading to a strategic *choice* of an *action* directed toward an *objective.* This thought process is graphically outlined in Figure 11.1.

In Figure 11.1, the large circle represents your skin, the boundary between your "inner" world and the "outer" world. The *stimulus* enters you through perception (seeing, hearing, touching). It arouses a response in you that touches on some need; it excites or frightens or pleases or angers you, and this is your *attitude* toward it. At this

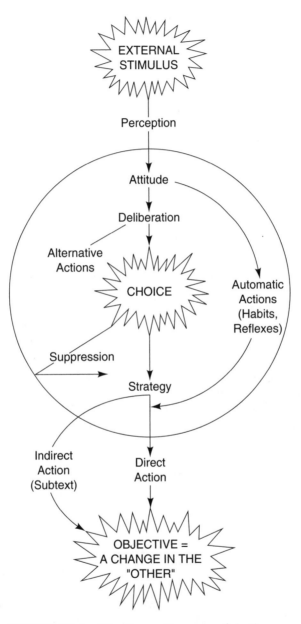

FIGURE 11.1 **The Inner Process of Action**

point, it may become an *automatic action,* or it may generate a *strategic choice.* The chosen action may then be either *direct, indirect,* or *suppressed.* Let's look at each step in this process.

THE STIMULUS

Actors sometimes do things without really responding to their stimulus. They only pretend to hear or see what is said or done to them because they fear that if they let the other characters truly affect them, they will lose control of their performance. They prefer the safety of reacting only to their own idea of what is happening.

For example, in *Death of a Salesman,* the actor playing Willy has to allow his growing desperation to come from the way in which the actor playing Howard avoids him. If instead he plays only his own idea of Willy's desperation, the scene will lack the immediacy and specificity of a real event. Likewise in the *Cheers* scene, Carla must be led by Ben to realize why she doesn't want to marry him. If she doesn't respond to him, the moment will feel like a "set up" instead of a spontaneous self-insight. Her lovely speech about her dream guy must be a realization that she had just at this moment, even though she has had the dream for years.

Thus, actors have to depend on each other to provide what everyone of them—and the scene itself—needs to move the story forward, moment by moment, as a real human event. Although this doesn't always happen, we always try to achieve this ideal working relationship. Don't let fear turn you into a hermetically sealed actor. Remember: Acting is not so much doing things as it is allowing yourself to be *made* to do them. Again, *acting is reacting!*

AUTOMATIC ACTIONS

As in real life, dramatic characters often act out of habit or impulse without conscious choice. In such cases, the stimulus leads directly to external action (see the arrow going around choice in Figure 11.1). This is what Stanislavski called *automatic* action. When the slap in the Impulse Circle was moving quickly, it was an automatic action, something you did without thinking.

For example, at one point in our sample scene, Willy loses his temper, yells at Howard, and bangs his hand on the table. Howard walks out. As soon as Howard is gone, Willy realizes that he has made a terrible mistake, and says "My God, I was yelling at him! How could I!" It was that thoughtless, impulsive, *automatic* action of anger that made it certain that Willy would be fired.

When approaching a part, it is extremely useful to identify the automatic aspects of your character's behavior as soon as possible. You will want to strive conscientiously to recreate the character's habits in yourself (for purposes of playing of the role only, of course). Allow sufficient time to immerse yourself into the character's instinctive world. Much of a character's behavior is habitual: voice, walk, mannerisms, any special skills or physical qualities—all contribute to the character's appearance. This body language must become as natural and habitual to you as it is to your character. In this, there is no substitute for practice.

Exercise 11.1: Automatic Actions

Review your scene with your partner; consider the things your character does without thinking about them; the way he or she talks, walks, moves, any particular habits, and so on. What do these things tell you about your character? What can you do to develop these habits in yourself for this role?

CHOICE

If an action is not automatic, then conscious thought is required. In Figure 11.1, you see that the first step in the thought process is to consider various things you might do. During this *deliberation,* one course of action is chosen and others are rejected. In order to fully experience this process, you need to create the alternative choices which your character rejects. In other words, it may be as important for you to decide what actions your character *would not choose* as it is to know those that he or she *would choose.*

After you have considered alternatives, you make your *strategic choice* about the best way to proceed in the given circumstances. This choice is at the center of the process. Before the choice, energy is moving *into* you; after the choice, energy is moving *out* of you. In other words, *choice is the point at which reaction turns into action.* Because choice is the moment at which reaction turns into action, it is the essence of drama. The most suspenseful moments in stories occur when a character confronts a significant and difficult choice and we wonder "what will he or she do?"

Choice is also the most revealing point in the process of action. In the making of significant choices, your character is expressing a microcosm of needs, ways of seeing the world, relationships, beliefs, and values. If you can experience all the factors influencing your character's most significant choices, you will be in touch with everything needed to create the character's mind.

Perhaps more important, your experience of your character's significant choices is the main way the *magic if* produces transformation. When you have entered into your character's circumstances and felt the same needs, and then made the same choices given those needs in those circumstances, action will follow naturally and with it will come transformation.

Of course, not every choice your character makes is to be given the weight of the significant choices we have been discussing here. In a typical scene, there will be only one or two such significant choices; in an entire role, there may be one singular choice that stands out above all the rest. Every choice, however, deserves to be fully experienced in each rehearsal or performance. Follow this general rule about automatic and nonautomatic actions: Whatever your character *doesn't* need to think about needs to be automatic for you; whatever your character *does* need to think about, you must think through each and every time you perform the scene.

In the scene from *Cheers,* for example, Carla's main choice is to not marry Ben, whereas Ben's main choice is to accept Carla's rejection with grace. Everything that is said and done in the scene either leads to or flows from these two crucial choices.

Here is a more detailed example of the process of choice from *Death of a Salesman.* As Willy enters, he sees Howard playing with a new recorder. He tries to get Howard's attention, but Howard puts him off. Willy's inner thought process at this moment could be expressed as a "stream of consciousness" or *inner monologue* which might sound like this:

1. **Stimulus:** *What the heck is that thing Howard is fiddling with?*
2. **Attitude:** *He's more interested in that gizmo than he is in me.*
3. **Alternatives:** *I could interrupt him and insist that he pay attention.*
4. **Choice:** *No, that might make him angry. I'll pretend to be interested in that thing. That'll get my foot in the door.*

5. **Action:** "What's that, Howard?"
6. **Objective:** *To get his attention in a way that ingratiates me to him.*

You can see that Willy's needs, values, way of thinking, way of relating to the world—in short, his entire psychology—is involved and expressed in each step of this mental process.

WORKING WITH INNER ACTION

The highly detailed view of your character's inner thought process we have explored so far is useful for understanding the principles involved. It may help you to solve specific problems when you have trouble understanding your character's thinking. There may also be a few extremely important moments in your role that, when examined in such detail, can help you understand the character better in general. Such a detailed approach, however, is too cumbersome to use while actually working on a role day to day. By simplifying the process, you can achieve an easy formula that you can apply as you actually work.

Try to break the process into three basic steps: the stimulus, need, and attitude forms the first step, which is called *arousal;* the consideration of alternatives and the choice of a course of action is the second step, which constitutes the *reaction;* finally, the initiative itself directed toward your objective, the third step, is called the *action.* So your inner process can be summarized by three key words:

Arousal–Reaction–Action

You can apply this system by asking yourself three questions about each of the transactions in a scene, just as in the following exercise.

Exercise 11.2: Choices (First Rehearsal off Book)

A. Working on your own, answer these questions about each of your character's actions in your scene.
   1. What am I reacting to?
   2. What does it make me want?
   3. What do I do to get it?
B. Choose the two most significant choices your character makes in the scene and examine each in detail: What do you learn about the character in general from these choices?

C. For the two most important choices, create the "inner monologue" or stream of thought which expresses your character's mental process. Your inner monologue might sound something like, "Look at that smug smile! He's not buying it at all. Maybe I could appeal to his vanity...." You might even write down the inner monologue.

D. Rehearse your scene with your partner. Take the time to experience each choice fully.

E. Perform the memorized scene for the group and critique it.

OBJECTIVES AND ACTIONS

A baseball batter rehearses his stance, grip, swing, and breathing; he studies the opposing pitchers; at the plate, he takes note of the wind and the position of the fielders. As he begins to swing at a pitch, however, he ceases to be aware of all these things and focuses his total awareness on the ball. This single objective channels all his energy into his action, the swing. Having this single objective allows the batter to synthesize all his other concerns, and all his rehearsed and intuitive skills, into a single complete action of mind and body.

For you as an actor, the "ball" is your character's objective, that is, what he or she is trying to accomplish at any given moment. Your focus on this single objective at the moment of action will overcome self-consciousness and give you power and control. In this Step, you will learn how to define your character's objectives (what he or she wants) and actions (what that person does to get it) in the most useful way.

DEFINING USEFUL OBJECTIVES

Experience has proven that objectives become more effective when they have three main qualities:

1. An objective needs to be *singular* because you wish to focus your energy on one thing rather than diffuse it by trying to do several things at once. Imagine a batter trying to hit two balls at the same time!

2. The most useful objective is in the immediate future, something you want *right now*. Although your character's needs may be rooted in the past, his or her action is directed toward an objective in the immediate future.

3. Finally, an objective must be *personally important* to you. As you have already learned, you must personalize it.

It is easy to remember these three requirements by the acronym "SIP:" *singular, immediate,* and *personal.*

Let's examine an objective from a scene to see how these principles are applied. In our sample scene from *Death of a Salesman,* Willy has an overall *scene objective* of wanting to get assigned to a territory closer to home. He has to pursue this scene objective, one step at a time, through *immediate objectives.* When he enters, he sees Howard playing with a new recorder. Therefore, Willy's immediate objective is to get Howard to stop what he is doing and *to pay attention.*

This objective is *singular* and *immediate.* It is also supremely important in a *personal* way to Willy: if he can't get Howard's attention, he won't be able to ask for a job in town, he won't be able to be a successful salesman, and he won't think of himself as a valuable human being. His deepest, lifelong need lives in the present moment, giving it all the urgency of a life-and-death struggle.

Once you have formed an objective that is SIP, you enter into action, either by doing, by saying, or both, directed toward that objective. Let's now see how to describe action in the most useful way possible.

PLAYABLE ACTIONS

While you are learning to act, it may help you to form verbal descriptions of your objectives and actions. Remember, however, that these verbal descriptions are valuable only insofar as they contribute to your actual experience of playing the scene. The ability to describe something comes from the analytical left side of the brain. The creative work of performance, however, originates from the intuitive right side of the brain. Although they can complement and augment one another wonderfully, the two sometimes get in each other's way. Nevertheless, learning to describe an action can help you to understand the qualities that make actions useful.

You want to define your actions in the most "playable" (that is, *active*) way possible. First, you use a *simple verb phrase in a transitive form,* that is, a verb that involves a *doing* directed *toward* someone else, such as "to flatter him." Since your energy must continually flow outward into the scene in order to keep the story moving, you avoid forms of the verb *to be* because this verb has no external object and its energy turns back on itself. You are never interested, for example, in "being angry" or "being a victim"; these states of being are not playable. Strive instead for a *doing* in which your energy flows toward an external object.

Next, you select a verb that carries a sense of the particular *strategy* chosen by your character to achieve the objective. As in real life, your character will naturally select an action that seems to offer the greatest chance for success in the given circumstances and in relation to the other person in the scene.

Let's return to the Willy Loman scene and see how you might describe your action if you were playing Willy. You have just entered; you desperately need to get a spot in town; you see Howard playing with the recorder. At this moment, you have the SIP objective of wanting Howard *to pay attention,* but you want to do it in a way that will make him feel positively towards you. As a salesman, you instinctively appeal to something the "client" is interested in, so you flatter him by praising the recorder and the stupid recording he has made of his family. The most complete description of your action and objective at this moment is *to flatter Howard by praising the recorder* (strategy) in order *to get him to pay attention to you in a positive way* (objective).

Exercise 12.1: Defining Objectives and Actions

Go through your scene and define each of your objectives and actions.

1. Make each objective SIP.
2. Describe each action with a transitive verb that expresses the strategy being used.

DIRECT AND INDIRECT ACTION: SUBTEXT

We have already seen that a character will select an action with the best chance for success in the given circumstances. As in real life, characters will often select a direct action such as persuading, demanding, cajoling, or begging. However, when there is an obstacle to direct action, the character will, as people do in everyday life, try to get around the obstacle through an indirect approach. An obstacle to direct action may be *internal*, like Willy's fear of angering Howard, or *external*, like Howard's obsession with the recorder.

When we act indirectly, we say or do one thing but really mean another. Although Willy *seems* to be enjoying Howard's recording, he actually wants to get Howard to turn it off and pay attention. This kind of "hidden agenda" creates a *subtext,* because there is a difference between the surface activity (the text) and the hidden objective (the subtext).

How do you play a subtext? Notice that the writer has provided a surface activity through which the subtext may be expressed—in this case, your feigned interest in the recorder. You must accept this surface activity as your immediate action: Do not attempt to bring the subtext to the surface! Doing so will destroy the reality of the scene. For one thing, if the audience can see Willy's subtext, they will wonder why Howard can't. Your simple awareness of subtext is enough, and often subtext will work even if you are unaware of it.

Trust the audience to deduce the subtext from the situation. It is part of the fun for the audience to figure these things out for themselves; if you make it obvious, they won't get to use their imagination!

NOT DOING

There is always at least one alternative available to a character in any situation, and that is the choice to *not* act, to suppress or delay action. Although we often think of "doing nothing" as a passive act, it can actually be a strong form of action. In our sample scene, for instance, it is hard for Willy to hold back as he tries to manipulate Howard toward the best possible moment to make his request.

Sometimes a character will even choose to do nothing even though the need is great, leaving the conflict or need unresolved even after the scene is over. This strategy builds suspense because it takes more effort to hold a strong impulse in than it would to let it out. As you can see in Figure 11.1, when a character chooses to suppress an impulse, that unresolved energy is reflected back into that character and builds up to become a source of increasing dynamic tension.

In everyday life we call this behavior *suppression,* which literally means "pushing down." Viewed in this way, there are no passive characters on the stage or screen, there are only characters who are aroused but then choose not to act. The choice to not act is a strong and playable action. To play a "not doing," identify what the character *wants* to do but *doesn't.* Let yourself feel the need to act strongly, and feel also the effort required to suppress the action. This process turns the "not doing" into a "doing" and makes it playable and dramatic.

Exercise 12.2: Subtext and Suppression

Work through your scene with your partner. Look for any indirect or suppressed action. Discuss each.

1. Why can't the actions be expressed directly or let out?
2. What surface activity has been provided through which they may be expressed?

Rehearse your scene with this awareness: avoid playing the subtext or the suppressed action.

CONNECTING ACTION WITH OTHERS

Since plays, films, and TV shows are about people interacting with one another, you must understand your objectives in ways that not only energize and focus you by being SIP and transitive, but which also connect you with the other characters in the scene. The best way to achieve connectedness is to think of your objective as being *in* the other character, something specific you need from that person.

The best objective, then, is *a change you want to bring about in the other character.* In life, when we do something to try to make a change in someone else, we watch to see if what we are doing is working; if it is not, we try something else. This should be true on stage as well. Ask yourself, "How would I know I was achieving my objective? What changes might I see in the other character that indicate that my approach is working?"

This sort of observable change that you want to bring about in the other character is the best way to define your objective. One great teacher even encouraged his actors to think of this as "a change in the other character's eyes." In the Willy Loman scene, for instance, your first objective might be "to get Howard to look at me with interest." Your full attention is on him, watching to see if your behavior is indeed producing the desired effect, or whether you might have to try a different approach (which eventually you do).

Exercise 12.3. Connecting the Action (Second Rehearsal)

Go through your scene and define each of your objectives as a change in the other character. Rehearse the scene with this awareness. Did you achieve a stronger interaction? Did the action of the scene flow better?

Step 13

BEATS AND SCENE STRUCTURE

Like people in everyday life, dramatic characters will pursue an action until it either succeeds or fails. If the action succeeds and they achieve their objective, they move on to a new objective. If they decide their action is not working, they may give up on their objective altogether, or they may redefine it. Most often, however, they will keep their objective and try a different strategy to achieve it.

For example, in our sample scene from *Death of a Salesman,* Willy begins the scene with the *scene objective* of getting a new territory. As Howard resists him, he tries a number of different strategies to achieve this objective, each of which is a new action. When he is fired, he must form a new objective, *to get his job back,* and he tries various strategies to accomplish this. Each change in his action can be felt as a change in the scene; each creates what Stanislavski called a new *unit of action.* Actors usually call these units of action *beats.*

Here is a simple exercise to experience a single unit of action.

Exercise 13.1: A Dramatic Breath

A. Take a single, complete breath that is as dramatic as you can make it. Don't think about it, just do it!

B. Try another; make it even more dramatic.

C. Discuss the things you did to make the breath more dramatic. Was there something that everyone did?

When trying this exercise for the first time, most people exaggerate their breath, making it louder and more visible. This, however, serves only to make the breath more "theatrical," not necessarily more *dramatic*. Consider for a moment those situations in real life which are naturally dramatic. What, for example, makes for a really dramatic basketball game?

First, the game must be important; the more significant the game, the higher the drama. Second, the outcome must be in doubt; the more evenly matched the teams are, the greater the drama. Third, the situation must continue to build toward a climax; and the longer it builds, the greater the drama. If one team gets too far ahead, suspense dies; but if the suspense can last to the very last shot, the drama is tremendous. So this is our definition of a dramatic event: *an important situation with the outcome in doubt and building in suspense.*

The moment of greatest suspense, when the outcome of a dramatic event hangs in the balance, is called the *crisis,* which literally means "turning point." Everything that happens before the crisis leads up to it with *rising* energy, whereas everything after the crisis flows naturally from it with *falling* energy. This is the fundamental shape of all dramatic events: a *conflict* which builds up suspense leads to a *crisis* and is then followed by a resolution. Usually, the resolution takes the form of a remarkable event, either comic or tragic, which ends the underlying conflict. In drama, this remarkable event is called the *climax* (see Figure 13.1).

Let's apply this definition of drama to the single "dramatic" breath you took in the last exercise. First, did you make the breath more

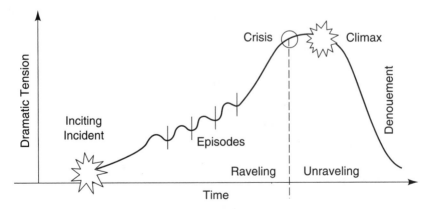

FIGURE 13.1   The Shape of Drama

"important" by taking in more air than usual, thus increasing the amount of energy involved? Next, did you increase suspense by holding your breath and building toward a crisis? As you held it, someone watching might wonder, "how long can this person hold it?" The longer you held it, the more the suspense built, until finally you exhaled. The crisis was the moment just before you decided to exhale, and the exhaling was the climax of the breath. Try the exercise again with this awareness.

A single beat is like this dramatic breath. It is *a unit of action in which one main issue is at stake, leading up to a crisis when that issue is decided.*

For example, the main issue in the first beat in the scene from *Death of a Salesman* is whether Willy will be able to get Howard's attention. Suspense builds until the crisis occurs, as Howard finally pays attention to him and says "Say, aren't you supposed to be in Boston?" The end of one beat is also the beginning of another, and so the moment when the change of action occurs is called a *beat change*. Either character may initiate the change. When the new beat begins, we feel a change in the direction and rhythm of the scene.

Willy goes on to try several more actions to get his old territory back from Howard and each is a beat change: He tries flattery, and when that doesn't work he appeals for sympathy; when that fails, he appeals to Howard's sense of loyalty, and then tries to make Howard feel guilty; finally he grows angry and demands justice; but when even that fails, he ends up begging. Even though Willy never changes his overall objective, each of his strategic actions is abandoned as it fails. Each shift in action is a "beat change" and moves the scene into a new direction.

LEVELS OF ACTION

Individual units of action connect to form larger patterns, producing *levels of action*. Because this is an idea more easily understood by the muscles than the mind, let's try a physical exercise to experience what we mean by *levels of action*.

Exercise 13.2: Levels of Action

Perform each of the following actions and experience the dramatic potential of each. Remember to focus on the crisis in each pattern: treat all that come before as leading up to the crisis, and all that follow as flowing from it.

1. A single step. Where is the crisis of a step? To intensify the experience, involve your breath by inhaling during the rising action, holding the breath during the crisis, and exhaling during the climax.

2. Experiment with differently shaped steps: a long rise, a long crisis, and a quick release; then a short rise, a short crisis, and a long release.

3. Take three steps and try to experience them as one phase, with the crisis in the third step. The first two steps still have mini-crises of their own, but now they lead up to the main crisis in the third step. Again, let your breath parallel the larger pattern.

4. Now try nine steps divided into three patterns of three steps each, with the crisis of this larger pattern in the last group. Try it again with the crisis in the first group of steps. Invent patterns of your own; add sound.

In this exercise you experienced how small units of action (like breaths or steps) can form a larger pattern of action having a shape of its own. Likewise, these larger phases can be connected into still larger patterns, which again have shapes of their own. On all these levels, the fundamental shape of rise, crisis, and release is the same, even though the proportion of the parts may be different (see Figure 13.2).

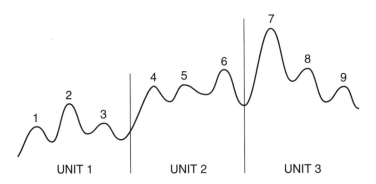

FIGURE 13.2   Compound Action. Here, nine steps divided into three units go together to produce one larger pattern.

All parts of a play or screenplay, even the tiniest bits, serve a function in regard to the whole. The "smallest" units of action, the individual transactions between characters, are called *moments* (in our sample scene, the first moment happens when Willy enters and asks Howard to "have a little talk," but Howard tells him to wait). Moments work together to form *beats,* each of which has a crisis (the first beat in our sample scene ends when Howard finally pays attention to Willy and asks, "Say, aren't you supposed to be in Boston?"). The beats work together to form a *scene,* which has a crisis of its own (in our examples, the crisis occurs when Howard decides to fire Willy). Finally, the scenes flow together to lead us to the crisis of the entire story (when Willy decides to commit suicide and drives away in his car).

Now apply this concept to the entire scene from *Death of a Salesman* on your own. Read through it again and see if you can feel where the beat changes occur. Make a mark at the point you feel each beat change. When you are done, compare your analysis with the breakdown following on page 88.

SCENE STRUCTURE

Rehearsing a scene is much like making a map of an unknown territory. You and your partners, through trial and error, explore it to find the pathway of action which the author has hidden beneath the surface of the dialogue. Each beat change is a turning point in the journey leading to the destination, the scene crisis. Once you and your partner have found a shared sense of the scene's structure, it will live as an underlying rhythm in the flow of the scene, you will feel the energy building beat by beat toward the crisis.

As your exploration of the scene in rehearsal develops, you begin to feel how the sequence of objectives and actions has a logical flow which can carry you through the scene with a natural momentum. Stanislavski called this sequence of objectives and actions the *score* of the role and considered it extremely important:

> *With time and frequent repetition, in rehearsal and performance, this score becomes habitual. An actor becomes so accustomed to all his objectives and their sequence that he cannot conceive of approaching his role otherwise than along the line of the steps fixed*

in the score.... The score automatically stirs the actor to physical action.[1]

This sense of the underlying structure of the scene will help you in many ways. For one, it will make it easy to learn your lines. As one of my actor friends says, he likes "to learn the action before he learns the words."

Your understanding of scene structure is especially important in single-camera film, where the scene is shot in small pieces—sometimes not in sequence—and assembled later. Usually, a section of the scene is shot from an overall point of view; this is called the *master.* Closer individual shots are then made, called *coverage,* which are later to be inserted into the master by the editor. Since several takes of each are usually required, the whole process can take many hours. Your performance must be consistent from take to take. Your close-ups must match the master as to timing, position, expression, and so on. This means that the film actor must have a firm sense of the structure of the scene, and how every moment fits into it.

In both film and stage work, then, a good sense of scene structure is the "map" which permits all the actors to support one another in their journey through the scene. The "map" helps to lessen your fear of becoming lost, making your work more playful and creative; it also helps you to experience the scene as a single, rhythmic event. One symptom that the scene has started to "play" in this way is that it will seem shorter to you when you perform it. It is this natural flow of the action that we call good *pace.*

SCENE BREAKDOWN

An analysis of the structure of a scene, beat by beat, is called a *scene breakdown.* As an example of a breakdown, let's again examine the sample scene from *Death of a Salesman;* compare what follows to the breakdown that you have already done on your own.

Beat One: Willy, unable to go on driving as much as his job requires, visits his new boss, Howard. Willy enters somewhat hesitantly

---

[1]Stanislavski, *Creating a Role,* p. 62.

and finds Howard playing with a new toy, a recorder. Howard wants to avoid this unpleasant confrontation (we learn later that he has already decided to fire Willy and has been putting it off), so he goes on playing with the recorder and forces Willy to listen to inane recordings of his family. Like a good salesman, Willy listens dutifully and even flatters Howard, while trying four times to bring up the reason for his visit. The conflict in this beat is between Willy's action of *getting Howard's attention by flattery,* versus Howard's counterobjective of *avoiding Willy by playing with the recorder.* The crisis is finally reached when Howard counterattacks by asking, "Say, aren't you supposed to be in Boston?"

Beat Two: in this short beat, Howard attacks by demanding to know, "What happened? What're you doing here?" Willy reacts weakly, but manages to state his case: "I've come to the decision that I'd rather not travel anymore." He reminds Howard that he had promised to find him "some spot for me here in town," but Howard responds, "Well, I couldn't think of anything for you, Willy." The main conflict of the scene is now on the table: Willy must get off the road, but Howard refuses to help.

Beat Three: This beat might be defined as three mini-beats, three quick thrusts of different strategies by Willy: appealing to sympathy ("I'm just a little tired"), appealing to loyalty ("I was with the firm when your father used to carry you in here in his arms"), and then demanding his right (*with increasing anger*); Howard parries each of these thrusts. What unifies this beat, however, is Willy's action of *bargaining,* as he steadily lowers the salary he is willing to accept in return for a spot in town.

Beat Four: Willy tries to make Howard understand by telling him how he decided to become a salesman, and even lowers his price to forty dollars a week, but Howard responds, "Kid, I can't take blood from a stone."

Beat Five: Willy grows desperate and demands justice, reminding Howard of his thirty-four years with the firm and the promises Howard's father had made. Howard simply walks out: "You'll have to excuse me, Willy, I gotta see some people. Pull yourself together."

Beat Six: Willy, now alone, thinks that he sees his old boss sitting in his chair, and is then frightened by accidentally turning on the recorder (which symbolizes Willy's inability to deal with the changes in the world).

Beat Seven: Howard reenters, and Willy, knowing that he has made a terrible mistake, tries to fix things by saying, "I'll go to Boston." The scene is now at its *main crisis.* Howard fires Willy: "Willy, you can't go to Boston for us."

Beat Eight: Willy starts to beg, but Howard refuses to take responsibility, and asks, "Where are your sons? Why don't your sons give you a hand?" Of course, the last thing a proud man like Willy will do is to accept help from his sons.

As you see, a breakdown greatly simplifies the scene for you. This fairly long scene (some ten minutes of playing time) can be understood as consisting of six individual beats leading to its main crisis, followed by one beat of follow-through.

Most important, notice that within each beat each character has *a single objective and action.* This permits you to translate the structure of the scene into the thoughts and actions of your character. You find the thought process that moves your character from objective to objective. Consequently, this sequence of objectives becomes the *score* of your role. You can see now that the score of your role is based directly on the structure provided by the writer: your sequence of objectives reflects the way your character helps move the scene, beat by beat, toward its crisis.

Having understood the structure of the scene, and having developed the score of your role which is based on it, you are free to play the scene and surrender your awareness to the character's immediate objectives, letting the score carry you through the scene, secure in the knowledge that what your character thinks, says, and does will move the story toward its ultimate destination.

Exercise 13.3: Scene Breakdown (Third Rehearsal)

A. Working with your partner, come to a mutual agreement about where the overall crisis of the scene happens. Then do a scene breakdown by agreeing on where each beat change happens.

B. On your own, define your character's action and objective in each beat, whether you initiate the beat change or not.

    1. Remember to express each action as a transitive verb that is "SIP" (singular, immediate, and personally important).

    2. Try to think of each objective as a desired change in the other character.

C. Rehearse the scene together to clarify the rhythms of the beat changes.

D. Begin to develop your score, seeing how each of your objectives contributes to the flow of the scene.

E. Read the scene in front of the group; ask the group to note where they feel the beats changing, and where they feel the crisis of the entire scene occurs. Afterward, compare their response to your breakdown.

Step 14

THROUGH-LINE
AND SUPEROBJECTIVE

You now understand that a good story is structured on levels of action: individual moments make up beats, beats make up scenes, and the scenes form the overall shape of rising and falling action by giving unity to the whole.

These levels of action relate directly to the inner life of your character. You will have an objective on each level: in each beat you have a *beat objective;* the objectives of the beats in sequence lead toward your *scene objective;* and your scene objectives can be seen as springing from a deep, overall objective which is your character's "life goal," his or her *superobjective.*

For example, consider again the scene from *Death of a Salesman.* Willy finds Howard engrossed in his new recorder; at this moment his *beat* objective is to get Howard's attention so he can move toward his *scene* objective of getting his old territory back. His scene objective is connected directly to his *superobjective:* to be a successful salesman, which for Willy is a way to prove himself a worthy human being in the eyes of others by earning money and respect. (Notice that defining the superobjective, as defining objectives on any level, requires using a transitive verb.)

If we follow each of Willy's beat and scene objectives throughout the play, we see how in each case he is led from objective to objective in pursuit of this superobjective. The logic of this sequence of objectives striving toward the superobjective is called the *through-line* of the role. Stanislavski described it like this:

> In a play the whole stream of individual minor objectives, all the imaginative thoughts, feelings and actions of an actor should con-

*verge to carry out this superobjective.... Also this impetus toward
the superobjective must be continuous throughout the whole play.*[1]

Stanislavski once said that each of a character's actions fits into the
through-line like vertebrae in a spine. Therefore, some actors call the
through-line the "spine" of the role.

Identifying your character's through-line of action as being driven
by the person's superobjective can help you to better understand each
of your specific actions, connecting each action to the character's
deepest needs and desires. It can also help you to see how the sequence
of objectives has a single driving force; thus you can "play through"
each moment and achieve both unity and momentum (good *pace*) in
your performance.

Your character's superobjective may be conscious or (more commonly) unconscious. If the character is unconscious of it, you—the
actor—will have to treat it in a special way. You will take it fully into
account as you work, but you will not let your knowledge as an actor
"contaminate" your character reality. Remember the idea of dual consciousness: what you know as the actor is not the same thing as what
your character knows. The great acting teacher Lee Strasberg once said
the hardest thing about acting "is not knowing what you know."

Whether your character is conscious of the superobjective, it functions as an underlying principle which affects all of your actions, and
establishes your attitude toward life. Willy Loman tries to earn self-
esteem through selling; he confuses success as a salesman with success
as a human being. Each moment, each beat, each scene, and every
aspect of Willy's psychology can be understood as reflecting this
superobjective. Eventually, he is no longer able to sell either his prod-
ucts or himself. His last "sale," then, is his suicide, making the insurance money his last "paycheck." Thus, this final, desperate act (which
is the climax of the play) is the fulfillment of Willy's tragically mis-
guided superobjective.

PERSONALIZING THE SUPEROBJECTIVE

Because the superobjective of most major characters is fairly "universal," it is usually not difficult to personalize. Like Willy Loman, we all

---

[1]Stanislavski, *An Actor's Handbook,* p. 56.

want to be thought of as worthy, and we can all "identify" with Willy, however much we can see that Willy's way of pursuing self-esteem is mistaken. However, it may be more difficult to find the superobjective of minor characters, since the writer has not provided much information about them. Here you can be inventive, so long as your understanding of the character enables you to accurately serve your dramatic function within the play as a whole.

It may be useful to examine your character's attitude toward himself or herself. The character's self-image expresses much about the person's superobjective and attitude toward life. Willy's superobjective is to prove himself worthy by earning money and respect, so his underlying self-image must be that he is *un*worthy as a human being. Much of his behavior seems perversely dedicated to proving his own unworthiness; the self-image is often a self-fulfilling prophecy.

Let's apply these ideas to your scene.

Exercise 14.1: Self-Image

A. What is your character's dominant self-image? Enter into your character's frame of mind and complete these phrases:

  1. The most beautiful part of my body is…
  2. Happiness to me is…
  3. The thing I most want to do before I die is…
  4. The ugliest part of my body is…
  5. The thing I like best about myself is…
  6. Pain to me is…
  7. My mother…
  8. The most secret thing about me is…
  9. I can hear my father's voice speaking through my own when I tell myself…
  10. Love to me is…
  11. If you could hear the music in me…
  12. I want my epitaph to be…

B. Immediately work through the scene and allow these feelings to effect what you do.

Although you may develop some idea about your character's superobjective before rehearsals start, it is dangerous to become too set in your thinking; these early ideas need to be tested. Ideally, the sense of superobjective will emerge gradually from your experience of the specific actions of your character. Let your sense of the superobjective be the *result* of your rehearsal exploration, not a *substitute* for it.

Again, avoid the temptation to indicate. It is never your aim to explain your superobjective to the audience. Your job is to create experience, not to explain behavior.

Exercise 14.2: The Superobjective (Fourth Rehearsal)

A. Examine your character's actions: Can you see a superobjective toward which the person is striving? Is the character conscious of it?

B. Define the superobjective using a transitive verb phrase.

C. Now consider ways of personalizing this superobjective, so that you feel it with the same intensity as does your character. You might even find a line from the play which sums it up: Willy Loman says, "Be liked and you will never want."

D. Rehearse, then perform your scene for the group. Discuss how the superobjective is expressed in it. Did you avoid indicating?

THE ELEMENTS
OF CHARACTERIZATION

You have come a long way toward creating your character by considering the *functional* traits the writer gave your character so this role could serve a particular purpose within the story believably. Now you will put on the "finishing touches" by exploring the *likeness* traits which "round out" the character.

We can classify all traits of character in four categories, as outlined here by Oscar Brockett:

> *The first level of characterization is physical and is concerned only with such basic facts as sex, age, size, and color. Sometimes a dramatist does not supply all of this information, but it is present whenever the play is produced, since actors necessarily give concrete form to the characters...*
>
> *The second level is social. It includes a character's economic status, profession or trade, religion, family relationships—all those factors that place him in his environment.*
>
> *The third level is psychological. It reveals a character's habitual responses, attitudes, desires, motivations, likes and dislikes—the inner workings of the mind, both emotional and intellectual, which precede action...the psychological is the most essential level of characterization.*
>
> *The fourth level is moral. Although implied in all plays, it is not always emphasized. It is most apt to be used in serious plays, especially tragedies.*[1]

---

[1]Oscar G. Brockett, *The Theatre: An Introduction,* 3rd ed. (New York: Holt, Rinehart and Winston, 1974), pp. 39–40.

Let's look briefly at each of these levels of characterization.

PHYSICAL TRAITS

The first level, the physical, is of primary importance to you since the external traits of body and voice communicate all the other levels of characterization to your audience. As Brockett pointed out, the writer will have specified the essential aspects of your character's physical traits: gender, age, and perhaps some indication of his or her appearance. For example, Arthur Miller says of Willy Loman, "He is past sixty years of age, dressed quietly... his exhaustion is apparent."

There are three main sources of this information: First, the stage directions or prefaces by the author. Second, traits described by other characters (of course, such descriptions may be distorted by the other character's viewpoint). Third, and most important, the bodily traits you can deduce that are required for the character to perform their physical actions believably, such as their bodily strength or weakness. Willy, for example, might literally be a "low" man.

Exercise 15.1: Physical Traits

Examine the entire script or play from which your scene comes; find clues to your character's bodily and vocal traits in stage directions or the statements of other characters. What do you think their body and voice might be like? Are there aspects of your own body and voice that might need to be modified to play this character?

SOCIAL TRAITS

The script may also provide basic information about the social traits of a character, such as educational and social background, status, and the type of work the person does. Some of these can be deduced from the context of the play, others you may wish to invent for yourself, if you are sure that they are consistent with the evidence of the script. We suggested, for instance, that Willy Loman was the son of immigrant parents and had to work through the Depression. We might also assume that he never finished school.

The most important social traits are the general and specific relationships your character has with the other characters in the play. Just as your personality is greatly influenced by those around you in everyday life, so dramatic characters can be understood only in relationship to the other characters in their world.

In fact, the common idea that the actor creates the character is not entirely true. It would be truer to say that the actors create *each other's* characters by the way they relate to one another. *Think less about creating your own character and more about creating the other characters by the way you relate to them, and you will end up creating yourself in the best possible way.* For example, in *Death of a Salesman,* Willy has a relationship with each person in the play: as father, husband, lover, neighbor, employee, and salesman. Each of these relationships reveals another aspect of Willy's character; his "I" is comprised of all of these "me's." The actors playing all these other roles each create a part of Willy, and so all must understand the contribution they make and cooperate if Willy is to live fully for the audience. The actors playing Ben, Charlie, Howard, and any of the other characters, can best create themselves by creating Willy.

It is also a good idea to make your characterization develop in a way that emphasizes the differences between your character and other characters in the story. In the scene from *Cheers,* for example, we can assume that Diane is college educated and perhaps from a rich family, whereas Carla barely finished high school and comes from a tough working-class background. The differences between them enrich their relationship and give them obstacles to overcome in dealing with one another, all of which make for a more satisfying dramatic experience.

Exercise 15.2: Social Traits

A. Examine the play for information about your character's social background. If no specific information is given, make the best guesses you can. Consider each of these:

 1. Childhood environment
 2. Educational background
 3. Socioeconomic and/or ethnic background
 4. Work experiences

B. Rehearse your scene with your partner: your aim in this rehearsal is to create each other by the way you relate to one another.

PSYCHOLOGICAL TRAITS

As Oscar Brockett pointed out, "the psychological is the most important level of characterization" because it justifies and motivates all the others. But this is not to say that the psychology of the characters is always the most important element of the story as a whole. In stories in which the plot or the ideas are the dominant elements, the psychology of the characters may serve merely to make the action believable. Conversely, in stories in which character is the most important element, the plot may be designed mainly to reveal the psychology of the character.

You have already done considerable work on your character's thought processes. Here are some additional questions about your character's mind.

Exercise 15.3: Psychological Traits

Consider the mental process of your character. Is the person:

1. Simple or complex?
2. Fast or slow?
3. Rigid or flexible?
4. Precise or vague?
5. Rational or intuitive?
6. Global or sequential?

Many of these qualities can be seen as belonging to either "right-brained" or "left-brained" people. Left-brained people tend to be more "rational" and think in linear, verbal, and logical terms. Right-brained people are more "intuitive" and think globally, in spatial and emotional terms. (Acting, by the way, is a whole-brain activity requiring both the analytical and verbal skills of the left brain *and* the intuitive and emotional skills of the right brain.) In the scene from *Cheers,* for example, the methodical Diane is clearly a left-brainer, whereas the impulsive Carla is a right-brainer. How would you describe your character? Is this person right- or left-brained?

MORAL TRAITS

The moral level of character refers to your character's values. This person's moral blueprint may include:

1. A sense of right and wrong
2. A sense of beauty

3. Certain religious beliefs
4. Specific political convictions

The moral aspect of character is rarely important in the case of minor characters or in comedy. When the moral aspect of a character *is* important, it will always relate directly to the thematic content of the play. The moral choice confronting Willy Loman, for example, carries the whole meaning of Arthur Miller's play: our society tends to erode spiritual values and self-esteem by emphasizing material values as measures of self-worth.

In the previous Step you defined your character's superobjective. Without knowing it, you were automatically bringing much of their morality into focus; after all, the superobjective and the means used to achieve it are the active expressions of your character's values.

Exercise 15.4: Moral Traits

Speaking as your character, answer the following questions:

1. I believe that when we die, we...
2. The greatest thing one person can do for another is...
3. The person I admire most is...
4. The person I detest most in the world is...
5. The ugliest thing I ever saw was...
6. The most beautiful thing I ever saw was...
7. The proper role of government is...
8. I am superstitious about...
9. After I die, I want to be remembered as someone who...

ECONOMY OF CHARACTERIZATION

We have examined each of four levels of characterization. Each works in relation to the others, although one or more may dominate. As Oscar Brockett explains:

A playwright may emphasize one or more of these levels. Some writers pay little attention to the physical appearance of their characters, concentrating instead upon psychological and moral traits;

other dramatists may describe appearance and social status in detail. In assessing the completeness of a characterization it is not enough merely to make a list of traits and levels of characterization. It is also necessary to ask how the character functions in the play. For example, the audience needs to know little about the maid who only appears to announce dinner; any detailed characterization would be superfluous and distracting. On the other hand, the principal characters need to be drawn in greater depth. The appropriateness and completeness of each characterization, therefore, may be judged only after analyzing its function in each scene and in the play as a whole.[2]

Actors sometimes try to treat the butler or maid who announces dinner as if they were the stars of the show, creating a disruptive distraction in the scene. This is not to say that the butler or maid should not be fully characterized; they should be as fully characterized *as they need to be* to fulfill their dramatic function. Economy of characterization means giving your character all the traits needed, but no more. An overly detailed performance is as distracting as an incomplete one.

---

[2]Brockett, pp. 39–40.

Step 16

FINAL REHEARSALS

Now that you are well into the rehearsal of your scene, you and your partner are beginning to shape and specify the transactions of action–reaction that will form, link by link, the chain that binds the scene together. As you feel the connectedness of every moment with every other moment, your through-line begins to emerge and the scene begins "to play," to flow under its own power. You no longer have to *make* things happen, you can *let* them happen. As a result, your scenes begin to feel simpler and shorter. Finding and perfecting these connections is the most important business of your final rehearsals.

Exercise 16.1: Making Connections

Work through your scene with your partner; either of you may stop the rehearsal at any point when you do not feel connected to the flow of the action, when your partner is not "making" you do what you must do next.

At each point of difficulty, examine the moments that led up to it; what cues do you need from your partner to induce your next action? Work together so that every moment of the scene grows organically out of the flow of action and reaction.

Note: Do not tell your partner what to do, ask for what you *need* instead. Leave it to your partner to provide it. You might say something like "I need to be more threatened by that," but leave it to your partner to determine how best to threaten you.

BLOCKING

Blocking is the way in which the characters move in relation to one another, to the set, or to the camera. Good blocking is much more than the creation of pleasing spatial arrangements; it must also reflect the relationship of the characters and the underlying action of the scene. Blocking expresses situations such as: Who is dominant at this moment in the scene? What space does this person control? Who is on the character's side? Who is on the attack? Who is retreating? When does the counterattack happen?

Although the sense of spatial relationship is artistically heightened on the stage and for the camera, it is based on the way people relate to one another spatially in everyday life. Look around you and observe how the poses and locations people have taken in the room reflect their relationships and attitudes. Note the contrast between a fellow who always sits slumped in his chair at the back of the room and the girl who sits upright in the front row, ready to jump in at any moment. Notice too how changes in relationship are reflected by movements we make, like the angry husband who slams the door or the wife who throws a skillet after him. These are the kind of impulses you will feel as you experience your action—they are the basis of your blocking. Let yourself move!

Exercise 16.2: Blocking

A. Spend a few days watching the "blocking" of everyday life; notice how attitude, relationship, and action are expressed in the way people place themselves in a room and move in relationship to each other.

B. Consider the blocking of your scene. Work with your partner to make it an effective expression of the relationship and action in the scene. Follow your impulses.

When you are working with a director, he or she may have various approaches to blocking. Some directors will preplan the blocking in detail, but most directors prefer that the actors provide the impulses which generate the blocking, with the director then editing them as needed. Regardless of what methods your director uses, your main responsibility is to *justify* your stage movement so that it grows out of an inner need or expresses your relationship toward the other characters in the scene. You may have to supply this justification in your own mind if your director provides a piece of blocking that feels awkward, although many times a director is using the blocking to tell you something about the action. If he or she asks you to "move into her," the director may really be saying "this is where you counterattack."

Blocking for film and television is a very critical matter. Here, movements are expressed not in feet but in inches. Once a shot has been established by the director and cameraman, strips of colored tape are placed on the floor to mark the exact position of each actor's feet. If there are movements within the shot, each interim destination is marked in the same way. As you do the scene, you must "hit your marks" exactly, without looking down. It can even matter which foot your weight is on, since the composition of the shot and the focus of the camera may require your head to be in a precise location at a precise time.

The nature of film also requires that your eye movements be "blocked;" that is, your look must extend to precisely the right place at the right time, since the apparent location of the other character must match the distance to the lens. If the "eye line" is not consistent in the various shots of a scene, it cannot be edited together. (The other actors will usually stand in the proper places next to the camera to give you your eye-lines; camera actors gladly serve one another in this way.)

As difficult as this sounds, even this kind of critical positioning becomes second nature after a time. As you develop your performance, be it for the camera or for the stage, the blocking will emerge and be incorporated as a natural part of your total action. By concentrating on what your character is doing, you will naturally make the correct movements to the correct locations without thinking.

SHAPING AND PACING

In this late stage of rehearsal, each beat change and the scene crisis are brought into sharp focus. Accordingly, the flow of action that connects these elements is established and smoothed to provide a sense of urgency, significance, rising dramatic tension, and the momentum we call good pace. (Note that "pace" refers to the *momentum* of the action, regardless of its "tempo," which refers to its *speed*.)

One important element of good pace is *cueing,* the way one character begins to speak after another has finished. In real life, if you and I are discussing something, I listen to you in order to understand the idea you are trying to express. When I have grasped that idea, I form my response and am usually ready to begin answering before you have actually finished your sentence. Listen to real-life conversations; do you hear how we actually overlap one another's speeches slightly, or at least are ready to respond before the other person has stopped talking? This is good "cueing." (In film acting, such slight overlapping is sometimes forbidden by technical considerations, although it may later be recreated by the editor.)

Exercise 16.3: Shaping and Pacing the Scene (Dress Rehearsal)

A. Examine your scene with your partner: Are all the beat changes and the scene crisis fully realized? Can you feel these as changes in the scene's rhythmic shape?

B. Together, find or create the aspects of the situation that provide the urgency or sense of deadline that will drive the scene's momentum:

   1. The physical environment: time, place, and so on

   2. The social environment: customs, the presence of others

   3. The situation: internal or external factors that create urgency or tension

   4. The conflict between you

C. Practice your listening and responding skills to produce good cueing.

D. After rehearsing your scene to achieve good shape and pace, perform it for your group. Ask your fellow students to signal whenever they feel the shape of the action becoming vague, or the pace dropping.

SPONTANEITY

What you do in performance should feel spontaneous, "as if for the first time," no matter how many times you have done it before. To achieve this spontaneity, you must keep your awareness on your objective rather than on the mechanics of your external action, just as the baseball batter thinks only about the ball and not about his swing. Otherwise you will only be "going through the motions," repeating the external aspects of your performance without re-experiencing the internal needs that drive the externals.

Notice that spontaneity does not mean that your performance is erratic or changeable: during the rehearsal process you gradually refine your external action until it becomes dependable, consistent, stageworthy, and automatic, just as the baseball batter has rehearsed all the aspects of his swing until he can do it without thinking. As Stanislavski said,

> *A spontaneous action is one that, through frequent repetition in rehearsal and performance, has become automatic and therefore free.*[1]

Because you are able to perform your action without thinking about it, your mind is free to concentrate fully on the objective and to experience your action "as if for the first time."

EMOTION IN PERFORMANCE

Young actors sometimes think they must recreate the character's emotion in order to generate each performance "truthfully," but this is an exhausting and unreliable way of working. Since emotion arises from action, you need only *do* what your character does and *think* the thoughts involved in the action; the performance itself will then give you the emotion.

We may sometimes be tempted to admire the emotionality of the actor who loses control and is overwhelmed, but the display of emotion for its own sake is never our true purpose. The great actor aspires to use emotional technique to realize the truth of the character according to the demands of the material. Stanislavski said it this way:

> *Our art... requires that an actor experience the agony of his role, and weep his heart out at home or in rehearsals, that he then calm himself, get rid of every sentiment alien or obstructive to his part. He then comes out on the stage to convey to the audience in clear,*

---

[1]Stanislavski, *An Actor's Handbook*, p. 138.

*pregnant, deeply felt, intelligible and eloquent terms what he has
been through. At this point the spectators will be more affected than
the actor, and he will conserve all his forces in order to direct them
where he needs them most of all: in reproducing the inner life of the
character he is portraying.*[2]

The important idea here is that in performance, "the spectators will
be more affected than the actor." This is necessary for several reasons.
First, strong emotion will interfere with your craftsmanship; as Stanislavski put it, "a person in the midst of experiencing a poignant emotional drama is incapable of speaking of it coherently."[3] Second,
emotions are unreliable when it comes to generating a performance
that must be done repeatedly and on schedule. Stanislavski used the
example of the opera singer who, at the moment the music requires
a certain note with a certain feeling, cannot say to the conductor, "I'm
not feeling it yet, give me four more measures." Finally, if your performance calls undue attention to itself because of your emotion, you
will have failed. As an audience member I am not here to watch you
weep; I am here to weep myself.

Exercise 16.4: Final Performance

Present your scene, as fully staged as you are able. Use simple rehearsal furniture and props, and dress appropriately. Experience
something of the thrill of an opening night.

---

[2]Stanislavski, *Building a Character*, p. 70.
[3]Ibid.

Afterword

THE POWER
OF TRANSFORMATION

Your sense of purpose is what will give you courage and power as an actor. It grows from your respect for your own talent, your love for the specific material you are performing, and your desire to use both to serve your audience. It is this drive to be *at service* through your art that will finally overcome the self-consciousness of your ego and carry you beyond yourself, giving you a transcendent purpose from which comes dignity, fulfillment, and ongoing artistic vitality.

Stanislavski called this ongoing artistic vitality "theatrical youthfulness." Near the end of his life he addressed a group of young actors with these words:

> *The first essential to retain a youthful performance is to keep the idea of the play alive. That is why the dramatist wrote it and that is why you decided to produce it. One should not be on the stage, one should not put on a play for the sake of acting or producing only. Yes, you must be excited about your profession. You must love it devotedly and passionately, but not for itself, not for its laurels, not for the pleasure and delight it brings to you as artists. You must love your chosen profession because it gives you the opportunity to communicate ideas that are important and necessary to your audience. Because it gives you the opportunity, through the ideas that you dramatize on the stage and through your characterizations, to educate your audience and to make them better, finer, wiser, and more useful members of society.*[1]

---

[1]Nikolai Gorchakov, *Stanislavski Directs* (New York: Funk & Wagnalls, 1954), pp. 40–41.

The art of acting has always had a very special service to render, one which has become increasingly important today. It is rooted in the actor's ability to transform, to become "someone else." At a time when many people feel more and more insignificant and impotent, the actor's ability to be "in charge" of personal reality can be a source of hope and inspiration to them. Just as a play may teach us something about who we are, the actor's ability to transform may teach us something about who we may *become*. Acting can be a celebration of our power to control our own destiny. When we realize this, we find a renewed sense of ethical and spiritual purpose that is a source of great energy and courage.

Appendix **A**

SAMPLE SCENE 1

FROM *DEATH OF A SALESMAN* BY ARTHUR MILLER[1]

[*Howard Wagner, thirty-six ... is intent on threading a recording machine and only glances over his shoulder as Willy appears.*]

Willy: Pst! Pst!

Howard: Hello, Willy, come in.

Willy: Like to have a little talk with you, Howard.

Howard: Sorry to keep you waiting. I'll be with you in a minute.

Willy: What's that, Howard?

Howard: Didn't you ever see one of these? Wire recorder.

Willy: Oh. Can we talk a minute?

Howard: Records things. Just got delivery yesterday. Been driving me crazy, the most terrific machine I ever saw in my life. I was up all night with it.

Willy: What do you do with it?

Howard: I bought it for dictation, but you can do anything with it. Listen to this. I had it home last night. Listen to what I picked up. The first one is my daughter. Get this.

---

[1] From *Death of a Salesman* by Arthur Miller. Copyright © 1949, renewed © 1977 by Arthur Miller [Dramatists Play Service version used]. Used by permission of Viking Penguin, a division of Penguin Books USA Inc.

[*He flicks the switch and "Roll out the Barrel" is heard being whistled.*]

Listen to that kid whistle.

Willy: Ts, ts. Like to ask a little favor if you...

[*The whistling breaks off, and the voice of Howard's daughter is heard.*]

His Daughter: "Now you, Daddy."

Howard: She's crazy for me! [*Again the same song is whistled.*] That's me! Ha! [*He winks.*]

Willy: You're very good!

[*The whistling breaks off again. The machine runs silent for a moment.*]

Howard: Sh! Get this now, this is my son.

His Son: "The capital of Alabama is Montgomery; the capital of Arizona is Phoenix; the capital of Arkansas is Little Rock; the capital of California is Sacramento..." [*and on, and on.*]

Howard [*Holding up five fingers*]: Five years old, Willy!

Willy: He'll make an announcer some day!

His Son [*Continuing*]: "The capital..."

Howard: Get that—alphabetical order!

[*The machine breaks off suddenly.*]

Wait a minute. The maid kicked the plug out.

Willy: It certainly is a—

Howard: Sh, for God's sake!

His Son: "It's nine o'clock, Bulova watch time. So I have to go to sleep."

Willy: That really is—

Howard: Wait a minute! The next is my wife.

[*They wait.*]

Howard's Voice: "Go on, say something." [*Pause.*] "Well, you gonna talk?"

His Wife [*Shyly, beaten*]: "Hello." [*Silence.*] "Oh, Howard, I can't talk into this..."

Howard [*Snapping the machine off*]: That was my wife.

Willy: That is a wonderful machine. Can we—

Howard: I tell you, *Willy,* I'm gonna take my camera, and my band-saw, and all my hobbies, and out they go. This is the most fascinating relaxation I ever found.

Willy: I think I'll get one myself.

Howard: Sure, they're only a hundred and a half. You can't do without it. Supposing you wanna hear Jack Benny, see? But you can't be at home at that hour. So you tell the maid to turn the radio on when Jack Benny comes on, and this automatically goes on with the radio...

Willy: And when you come home you...

Howard: You can come home twelve o'clock, one o'clock, any time you like, and you get yourself a Coke and sit yourself down, throw the switch, and there's Jack Benny's program in the middle of the night!

Willy: I'm definitely going to get one. Because lots of times I'm on the road, and I think to myself, what I must be missing on the radio!

Howard: Don't you have a radio in the car?

Willy: Well, yeah, but who ever thinks of turning it on?

Howard: Say, aren't you supposed to be in Boston?

Willy: That's what I want to talk to you about, Howard. You got a minute?

[*He draws a chair in from the wing.*]

Howard: What happened? What're you doing here?

Willy: Well...

Howard: You didn't crack up again, did you?

Willy: Oh, no. No...

Howard: Geez, you had me worried there for a minute. What's the trouble?

Willy: Well, tell you the truth, Howard. I've come to the decision that I'd rather not travel any more.

Howard: Not travel! Well, what'll you do?

Willy: Remember, Christmas time, when you had the party here? You said you'd try to think of some spot for me here in town.

Howard: With us?

Willy: Well, sure.

Howard: Oh, yeah, yeah. I remember. Well, I couldn't think of anything for you, Willy.

Willy: I tell ya, Howard. The kids are all grown up, y'know. I don't need much any more. If I could take home—well, sixty-five dollars a week, I could swing it.

Howard: Yeah, but Willy, see I—

Willy: I tell ya why, Howard. Speaking frankly and between the two of us, y'know—I'm just a little tired.

Howard: Oh, I could understand that, Willy. But you're a road man, Willy, and we do a road business. We've only got a half-dozen salesmen on the floor here.

Willy: God knows, Howard, I never asked a favor of any man. But I was with the firm when your father used to carry you in here in his arms.

Howard: I know that, Willy, but—

Willy: Your father came to me the day you were born and asked me what I thought of the name Howard, may he rest in peace.

Howard: I appreciate that, Willy, but there just is no spot here for you. If I had a spot I'd slam you right in, but I just don't have a single solitary spot.

[*He looks for his lighter. Willy has picked it up and gives it to him. Pause.*]

Willy [*With increasing anger*]: Howard, all I need to set my table is fifty dollars a week.

Howard: But where am I going to put you, kid?

Willy: Look, it isn't a question of whether I can sell merchandise, is it?

Howard: No, but it's a business, kid, and everybody's gotta pull his own weight.

Willy [*Desperately*]: Just let me tell you a story, Howard—

Howard: 'Cause you gotta admit, business is business.

Willy [*Angrily*]: Business is definitely business, but just listen for a minute. You don't understand this. When I was a boy—eighteen, nineteen—I was already on the road. And there was a question in my mind as to whether selling had a future for me. Because in those days I had a yearning to go to Alaska. See, there were three gold strikes in one month in Alaska, and I felt like going out. Just for the ride you might say.

Howard [*Barely interested*]: Don't say.

Willy: Oh, yeah, my father lived many years in Alaska. He was an adventurous man. We've got quite a little streak of self-reliance in our family. I thought I'd go out with my older brother and try to locate him, and maybe settle in the North with the old man. And I was almost decided to go, when I met a salesman in the Parker House. His name was Dave Singleman. And he was eighty-four years old, and he'd drummed merchandise in thirty-one states. And old Dave, he'd go up to his room, y'understand, put on his green velvet slippers—I'll never forget—and pick up his phone and call the buyers, and without ever leaving his room, at the age of eighty-four, he made his living. And when I saw that, I realized that selling was the greatest career a man could want. 'Cause what could be more satisfying than to be able to go, at the age of eighty-four, into twenty or thirty different cities, and pick up a phone, and be remembered and loved and helped by so many different people? Do you know? When he died—and by the way he died the death of a salesman, in his green velvet slippers in the smoker of the New York, New Haven, and Hartford, going into Boston—when he died, hundreds of salesmen and buyers were at his funeral. Things were sad on a lotta trains for months after that. [*He stands up. Howard has not looked at him.*] In those days there was personality in it, Howard. There was respect, and comradeship, and gratitude in it. Today, it's all cut and dried, and there's no chance for bringing friendship to bear—or personality. You see what I mean? They don't know me anymore.

Howard [*Moving away, to the right*]*:* That's just the thing, Willy.

Willy: If I had forty dollars a week—that's all I'd need. Forty dollars, Howard.

Howard: Kid, I can't take blood from a stone, I—

Willy [*Desperation is on him now*]*:* Howard, the year Al Smith was nominated, your father came to me and—

Howard [*Starting to go off*]*:* I've got to see some people, kid.

Willy [*Stopping him*]*:* I'm talking about your father! There were promises made across this desk! You mustn't tell me you've got people to see—I put thirty-four years into this firm, Howard, and now I can't pay my insurance! You can't eat the orange and throw the peel away—a man is not a piece of fruit! [*After a pause*]: Now pay attention. Your father—in 1928 I had a big year. I averaged a hundred and seventy dollars a week in commissions.

Howard [*Impatiently*]*:* Now, Willy, you never averaged—

Willy [*Banging his hand on the desk*]: I averaged a hundred and seventy dollars a week in the year of 1928! And your father came to me—or rather, I was in the office here—it was right over this desk—and he put his hand on my shoulder—

Howard [*Getting up*]: You'll have to excuse me, Willy, I gotta see some people. Pull yourself together. [*Going out*]: I'll be back in a little while.

[*On Howard's exit, the light on his chair grows very bright and strange.*]

Willy: Pull myself together! What the hell did I say to him? My God, I was yelling at him! How could I! [*Willy breaks off, staring at the light, which occupies the chair, animating it. He approaches this chair, standing across the desk from it.*] Frank, Frank, don't you remember what you told me that time? How you put your hand on my shoulder, and Frank… [*He leans on the desk and as he speaks the dead man's name he accidentally switches on the recorder, and instantly*]

Howard's Son: "…of New York is Albany. The capital of Ohio is Cincinnati, the capital of Rhode Island is…" [*The recitation continues.*]

Willy [*Leaping away with fright, shouting*]: Ha! Howard! Howard! Howard!

Howard [*rushing in*]: What happened?

Willy [*Pointing at the machine, which continues nasally, childishly, with the capital cities*]: Shut it off! Shut it off!

Howard [*Pulling the plug out*]: Look, Willy…

Willy [*Pressing his hands to his eyes*]: I gotta get myself some coffee. I'll get some coffee…

[*Willy starts to walk out. Howard stops him*]

Howard [*Rolling up the cord*]: Willy, look…

Willy: I'll go to Boston.

Howard: Willy, you can't go to Boston for us.

Willy: Why can't I go?

Howard: I don't want you to represent us. I've been meaning to tell you for a long time now.

Willy: Howard, are you firing me?

Howard: I think you need a good long rest, Willy.

Willy: Howard—

Howard: And when you feel better, come back, and we'll see if we can work something out.

Willy: But I gotta earn some money, Howard. I'm in no position to—

Howard: Where are your sons? Why don't your sons give you a hand?

Willy: They're working on a very big deal.

Howard: This is no time for false pride, Willy. You go to your sons and you tell them that you're tired. You've got two great boys, haven't you?

Willy: Oh, no question, no question, but in the meantime...

Howard: Then that's that, heh?

Willy: All right, I'll go to Boston tomorrow.

Howard: No, no.

Willy: I can't throw myself on my sons. I'm not a cripple!

Howard: Look, kid, I'm busy this morning.

Willy [*Grasping Howard's arm*]: Howard, you've got to let me go to Boston!

Howard [*Hard, keeping himself under control*]: I've got a line of people to see this morning. Sit down, take five minutes, and pull yourself together, and then go home, will ya? I need the office, Willy. [*He starts to go, turns, remembering the recorder, starts to push off the table holding the recorder.*] Oh, yeah. Whenever you can this week, stop by and drop off the samples. You'll feel better, Willy, and then come back and we'll talk. Pull yourself together, kid, there's people outside.

SAMPLE SCENE 2

FROM *CHEERS* BY TOM REEDER[2]

[Note: Carla works as a waitress in the Cheers bar. In this scene, Carla has just received an offer of marriage from Ben Ludlow, an eminent psychologist she has been dating. She has reacted strangely to the proposal and has gone into the back room to think. Diane follows her to see what's wrong.]

INT. POOL ROOM

Carla is standing lost in thought. <u>Diane enters</u>.

>   DIANE
>
>   Carla, I couldn't help noticing that
>   you're not exactly leaping for joy.
>   Bennett Ludlow is a wonderful catch.
>
>   CARLA
>
>   (WITH DIFFICULTY) There are things
>   he doesn't know about me.
>
>   DIANE
>
>   A little mystery is good for a
>   marriage. What haven't you told him?
>
>   CARLA
>
>   Well, I haven't been completely honest
>   about my kids.

---

[2]Excerpted from the episode entitled "Whodunit," written by Tom Reeder, from the television series *Cheers*, created by Glen Charles & Les Charles and James Burrows. Copyright 1984 Paramount Pictures Corporation. All Rights Reserved.

> DIANE

What haven't you told him about them?

> CARLA

That they live.

> DIANE

He doesn't know you have children?

> CARLA

Shhhhh!

> DIANE

Carla, you have to tell him. He's
going to wonder who those little
people are running around the house.

> CARLA

I'm hoping he'll be too polite to ask.

OFF DIANE'S LOOK.

> CARLA (CONT'D)

I didn't want to scare him off.

> DIANE

Seriously, Carla, it's only fair
that you tell him immediately that
you have five children.

> CARLA

Six.

> DIANE

Okay, six. But if you wait, if you put
this off—I thought it was five?

> CARLA

It was. But I just came from the doctor.

<u>DIANE GROANS WITH RECOGNITION.</u>

> ### DIANE
>
> Carla, when you took hygiene in high school, did you cut the "how-not-to" lecture?

> ### CARLA
>
> I had to. I was pregnant. I tell you I'm the most fertile woman who ever lived. For me there's only one method of birth control that's absolutely foolproof, but it makes me sick to my stomach.

> ### DIANE
>
> What's that?

> ### CARLA
>
> Saying no.

<u>LUDLOW ENTERS.</u>

> ### LUDLOW
>
> Carla, are you all right?

> ### DIANE
>
> Well, I'm going to go celebrate with the others. We're like a big family here at Cheers. You know what they say about a big family—more to love. I always say—

> ### CARLA
>
> Beat it.

> ### DIANE
>
> Bye.

<u>DIANE EXITS.</u>

LUDLOW

Carla, my proposal wasn't received
with the enthusiasm I expected it
to be. In fact, it occurred to me
that I never actually heard you say
"yes."

CARLA

I know. Benny, I have to tell you
some things about myself.

LUDLOW

This sounds serious.

CARLA

It is. Benny, have you ever seen
"The Brady Bunch?"

LUDLOW

Yes, I think so.

CARLA

Picture them with knives.

LUDLOW

I don't understand.

CARLA

I have five children.

LUDLOW

Five?

CARLA

Well ... five and counting. You're going to
be a daddy.

LUDLOW SITS DOWN.

LUDLOW

This is quite a day.

CARLA

You now have my permission to
withdraw the proposal.

LUDLOW

Do you want me to withdraw the
proposal, Carla?

CARLA

I want you to do what you want
to do.

LUDLOW

I want to marry you.

CARLA

You're kidding. Wow. What class.

LUDLOW

I still haven't heard you say yes.

CARLA

I know. (GENUINELY PUZZLED) Why do
you think that is?

LUDLOW

I think if you examine your
feelings, you'll know.

CARLA

Yeah, I guess I know. I love somebody else.

LUDLOW

Who?

CARLA

I don't know his name. I haven't
met him yet, but I've had this real
clear picture of him in my mind for
what seems like forever. He's going
to walk into this bar some night.
Actually, not walk. More like swagger.
You know, confident but not cocky.
He's okay-looking, but he's no pretty
boy. He's a swell dresser. He's wearing
this burgundy leather jacket. His nose
is broken in all the right places. He's
got this scar on his chin he won't talk
about. He cracks his knuckles all the
time. Drives me up the wall, but, what
can you do? Doesn't talk much. Doesn't
have to. He falls for me hard. I hurt
him a few times. He gets over it. We
get married.

SHE TURNS TO LUDLOW.

CARLA (CONT'D)

So you see, it would be kind of messy if I
was already married when he gets here.

LUDLOW

You know something, Carla? I sort of
have a dream girl myself.

CARLA

What's she like?

LUDLOW

She's a spunky, hearty, little
curly-haired spitfire, who doesn't
know what's good for her.

CARLA

I hope you find her some day.

LUDLOW

Me too. And I want you to know I intend to
take care of this child financially.

CARLA

You bet your buns you will, Benny
Baby.

HE EXITS. CARLA STANDS THERE CONSIDERING HER FATE.

Appendix B

USEFUL PLAYS

The following American plays are good sources of scenes with the qualities most useful for this book. Most of them are available in inexpensive paperback "acting editions" from the publishers indicated. There are also a number of anthologies of scenes for student actors on the market. One useful reference book, which indexes scenes in a variety of ways (male–male, female–male, female–female, and by genre and ethnicity), is *The Ultimate Scene and Monologue Source Book* by Ed Hooks (New York, Backstage Books), 1994.

After the Fall by Arthur Miller (Dramatists Play Service).

Ah, Wilderness! by Eugene O'Neill (Samuel French).

All My Sons by Arthur Miller (Dramatists Play Service).

Amen Corner, The by James Baldwin (Samuel French).

American Buffalo by David Mamet (Samuel French).

Andersonville Trial, The by Saul Levitt (Dramatists Play Service).

And Miss Reardon Drinks a Little by Paul Zindel (Dramatists Play Service).

Angels in America: Part I by Tony Kushner (Theatre Communications Group).

Anna Christie by Eugene O'Neill (Vintage Books).

Bedrooms: Five Comedies by Renee Taylor and Joseph Bologna (Samuel French).

Bent by Martin Sherman (Samuel French).

Birdbath by Leonard Melfi (Samuel French).

Born Yesterday by Garson Kanin (Dramatists Play Service).

Cat on a Hot Tin Roof by Tennessee Williams (Dramatists Play Service).

Chapter Two   by Neil Simon (Samuel French).

Chase, The   by Horton Foote (Dramatists Play Service).

Children's Hour, The   by Lillian Hellman (Dramatists Play Service).

Colored Museum, The   by George C. Wolfe (Broadway Play Publishing).

Come Back, Little Sheba   by William Inge (Samuel French).

Come Back to the 5 & Dime, Jimmy Dean, Jimmy Dean   by Ed Graczyk (Samuel French).

Coupla White Chicks Sitting around Talking, A   by John Ford Noonan (Samuel French).

Crimes of the Heart   by Beth Henley (Dramatists Play Service).

Crossing Delancey   by Susan Sandler (Samuel French).

Crucible, The   by Arthur Miller (Dramatists Play Service).

Dark at the Top of the Stairs, The   by William Inge (Dramatists Play Service).

Day in the Death of Joe Egg, A   by Peter Nichols (Samuel French).

Death of a Salesman   by Arthur Miller (Dramatists Play Service).

Death of Bessie Smith, The   by Edward Albee (Plume).

Delicate Balance, A   by Edward Albee (Samuel French).

Division Street   by Steve Tesich (Samuel French).

Duet for One   by Tom Kempinski (Samuel French).

Eccentricities of a Nightingale, The   by Tennessee Williams (Dramatists Play Service).

Effect of Gamma Rays on Man-in-the-Moon Marigolds   by Paul Zindel (Bantam).

Enter Laughing   by Joseph Stein (Samuel French).

Extremities   by William Mastrosimone (Samuel French).

Fences   by August Wilson (Samuel French).

Fool for Love   by Sam Shepard (Dramatists Play Service).

Frankie and Johnny in the Clair de Lune   by Terrence McNally (Dramatists Play Service).

Gingerbread Lady, The   by Neil Simon (Samuel French).

Glass Menagerie, The   by Tennessee Williams (Dramatists Play Service).

Glengarry Glen Ross   by David Mamet (Samuel French).

Golden Boy   by Clifford Odets (Dramatists Play Service).

Hatful of Rain, A   by Michael Vincente Gazzo (Samuel French).

Heidi Chronicles, The   by Wendy Wasserstein (Dramatists Play Service).

House of Blue Leaves, The   by John Guare (Samuel French).

Immigrant, The   by Mark Harelik (Broadway Play Publishing).

I Never Sang for my Father   by Robert Anderson (Dramatists Play Service).

I Ought to Be in Pictures by Neil Simon (Samuel French).

It Had to Be You by Renee Taylor and Joseph Bologna (Samuel French).

Last of the Red Hot Lovers by Neil Simon (Samuel French).

Last Summer at Bluefish Cove by Jane Chambers (JH Press).

Laundry and Bourbon by James McLure (Dramatists Play Service).

Lie of the Mind, A by Sam Shepard (Dramatists Play Service).

Little Foxes, The by Lillian Hellman (Dramatists Play Service).

Long Day's Journey into Night by Eugene O'Neill (Yale University Press).

Look Homeward, Angel by Ketti Frings (Samuel French).

Lost in Yonkers by Neil Simon (Samuel French).

Lovers and Other Strangers by Renee Taylor and Joseph Bologna (Samuel French).

Luv by Murray Schisgal (Dramatists Play Service).

Matchmaker, The by Thornton Wilder (Samuel French).

Middle Ages, The by A. R. Gurney, Jr. (Dramatists Play Service).

Moonchildren by Michael Weller (Samuel French).

Moon for the Misbegotten, A by Eugene O'Neill (Samuel French).

Murder at the Howard Johnson's by Ron Clark and Sam Bobrick (Samuel French).

Nerd, The by Larry Shue (Dramatists Play Service).

'Night, Mother by Marsha Norman (Dramatists Play Service).

Night of the Iguana, The by Tennessee Williams (Dramatists Play Service).

No Place to Be Somebody by Charles Gordone (Samuel French).

Odd Couple, The (Female Version) by Neil Simon (Samuel French).

Odd Couple, The (Male Version) by Neil Simon (Samuel French).

Of Mice and Men by John Steinbeck (Dramatists Play Service).

Oh Dad, Poor Dad, Mamma's Hung You in the Closet and I'm Feelin' so Sad by Arthur Kopit (Samuel French).

Only Game in Town, The by Frank D. Gilroy (Samuel French).

On the Open Road by Steve Tesich (Samuel French).

Philadelphia Story, The by Philip Barry (Samuel French).

Picnic by William Inge (Dramatists Play Service).

Prisoner of Second Avenue, The by Neil Simon (Samuel French).

Rainmaker, The by N. Richard Nash (Samuel French).

Raisin in the Sun, A by Lorraine Hansberry (Samuel French).

Red Coat, The by John Patrick Shanley (Dramatists Play Service).

Scenes from American Life by A. R. Gurney, Jr. (Samuel French).

Sea Horse, The   by Edward J. Moore (Samuel French).

Sexual Perversity in Chicago   by David Mamet (Samuel French).

Shadow Box, The   by Michael Cristofer (Samuel French).

Sign in Sidney Brustein's Window, The   by Lorraine Hansberry (Samuel French).

Six Degrees of Separation   by John Guare (Dramatists Play Service).

Speed-the-Plow   by David Mamet (Samuel French).

Splendor in the Grass   by William Inger (Dramatists Play Service).

Spoils of War   by Michael Weller (Samuel French).

Steel Magnolias   by Robert Harling (Dramatists Play Service).

Strange Snow   by Stephen Metcalfe (Samuel French).

Streetcar Named Desire, A   by Tennessee Williams (Dramatists Play Service).

Subject Was Roses, The   by Frank D. Gilroy (Samuel French).

Summer and Smoke   by Tennessee Williams (Dramatists Play Service).

Sweet Bird of Youth   by Tennessee Williams (Dramatists Play Service).

Tenth Man, The   by Paddy Chayefsky (Samuel French).

That Championship Season   by Jason Miller (Samuel French).

Time of Your Life, The   by William Saroyan (Samuel French).

To Gillian on Her Thirty-seventh Birthday   by Michael Brady (Broadway Play Publishing).

Touch of the Poet, A   by Eugene O'Neill (Random House).

Toys in the Attic   by Lillian Hellman (Dramatists Play Service).

Tribute   by Bernard Slade (Samuel French).

True West   by Sam Shepard (Samuel French).

Twice around the Park   by Murray Schisgal (Samuel French).

View from the Bridge, A   by Arthur Miller (Dramatists Play Service).

Vikings   by Stephen Metcalfe (Samuel French).

Waiting for Lefty   by Clifford Odets (Grove Press).

What I Did Last Summer   by A. R. Gurney, Jr. (Dramatists Play Service).

When You Comin' Back, Red Ryder?   by Mark Medoff (Dramatists Play Service).

Who's Afraid of Virginia Woolf?   by Edward Albee (Dramatists Play Service).

Women, The   by Clare Boothe Luce (Dramatists Play Service).

Zoo Story, The   by Edward Albee (Dramatists Play Service).

GLOSSARY

Action   Used in two ways. In a play or film script, the dramatic action is what happens in the story, scene, or beat in the most fundamental sense. For the actor, the action is what his or her character does to try to fulfill a need by winning some objective. Stanislavski spoke of both spiritual (inner) and physical (outer) action. Note that speaking is one of the most common forms of action; that is, a saying is also a doing. To be "in action" is to be totally involved in the task at hand and is the most desirable condition for the actor. Action is the most fundamental concept behind most systems of acting. (See also *Automatic action, Choice, Indirect action, Inner action, Justifying, Motivation, Objective, Reacting, Score, Stimulus, Strategy, Suppression,* and *Verb.*)

Ad lib   To insert words of your own into a script, usually on the spur of the moment.

AFTRA   The American Federation of Television and Radio Artists. The union that covers radio acting and some television shows that are not filmed. AFTRA will probably soon merge with the Screen Actors Guild. (See *SAG.*)

Agent   Someone who represents and markets actors. An agent normally gets a 10 percent commission on everything an actor earns. In film and television, actors are usually auditioned only when their names are submitted by a licensed agent, so getting an agent is often the first step in initiating a professional film or television career.

Attitude   The way your character feels about something that has happened.

Automatic action   Stanislavski's term for what we call a habit or reflex; something your character does without thinking.

Beat   A unit of action with its own specific conflict and crisis. In each beat a character has a single objective. Beats are formed of moments and flow to create the underlying structure of a scene. The term may have been created by someone with a Russian accent saying "bit" of action, though it makes sense as a unit of rhythm (as in "downbeat") because the flow of the beats is the primary rhythm of a scene.

Beat change   When one of the characters changes a strategy or objective, moving the scene in a new direction. A beat change results from either an automatic action or a deliberate choice made by one of the characters.

Believability   Something consistent with the created reality and style of the world of the story and the personality of the character, whether like everyday life or not.

Bio   (See *Resume.*)

Blocking   Establishing the positions and movements of the characters on the stage or in relation to the camera. Good blocking should express the underlying action of the scene. (See also *Mark.*)

Breakdown (See *Scenario.*)

Call   The time an actor is to report for work. Missing a call is a serious offense. In the theatre, calls are posted on the call board; in film and television, they are announced on a call sheet distributed near the end of each day's shooting for the following day.

Callback   There are usually preliminary auditions in the audition process from which a small number of actors are called back for a final audition.

Casting director   Preliminary auditions, especially in film and television, are usually conducted by a casting director who then selects the actors for callbacks with the director or producer. Casting directors are extremely important to actors starting out; they can be more important to the establishment of a career than are agents.

Cheating out   Standing so that your face is turned slightly toward the audience or camera. Cheating out is more important on stage than in film.

Choice   When pursuing a need, your character may consider several alternative courses of action and then make a strategic choice that appears to hold out the best chance of success. By examining your character's significant choices, you can gain a wealth of information about them.

Climax   The "main event," which is the resolution of the underlying conflict of a story and therefore ends the suspense. Scenes normally do not have climaxes, because the suspense of the story must carry into the next scene.

Continuity   In film and television, making sure that every detail of a shot matches the shots that precede or follow it. An actor has to be aware, for instance, of whether his or her right hand was over the left, how much liquid was in the glass, and so on. Continuity is the responsibility of the script supervisor, an unsung hero who remembers details like these even days later.

Costume parade   In the theatre, the first showing of the costumes on the set and under lights for approval by the director.

Coverage   In film, a scene is often shot from a wide perspective called the *master;* the camera is then repositioned for tighter shots called *coverage,* which the editor will later insert into the master. Consequently the actor's performance in coverage must match that of the master. Also the *close-ups,* which are the most demanding on the actors, are shot hours after the master, and actors must be careful to "save" something for them.

Crisis   The event in a story after which the outcome becomes, in hindsight, inevitable. Before this point, the energy of the story rises in suspense; during the crisis, the outcome hangs in the balance; and after the crisis, the energy flows toward resolution. While a crisis (or *turning point*) leads to a climax, it is not always the same thing as the climax and is often not the emotional high point of the story. A scene has a crisis in which the main issue of that scene is decided. A beat also has a crisis just before the beat change.

Cross   When the actor moves from point A to point B. Such movements need to be justified by some inner need. There are different kinds of crosses, such as the "banana," which is a slight curve so that the actor ends cheated out.

Cue   Anything that causes something to happen. For the actor, it refers to the line or event just before his or her character speaks or moves. It can also refer to one change in lighting or sound.

Cueing   The way in which one line follows another. In real life we often overlap one another in speech and begin responding slightly before the other person has finished speaking. In film, overlapping is sometimes avoided because it limits the editor's ability to cut from take to take. ("Cueing" also means helping actors learn or remember lines by prompting them, as in "Will you cue me?")

Cue-to-cue   A frustrating form of technical rehearsal in which the actors are asked to jump from light cue to light cue. To be avoided if at all possible, or conducted without the actors, because it is disruptive to the actors' experience of the rhythms of the scene.

Demonstration   Bertolt Brecht's idea that the actor does not "become" the character completely, but rather "demonstrates" the character's behavior for the audience while still expressing some attitude about it. Although this may sound like "indicating," the good Brechtian actor's passionate commitment to the ethical point being made gives the performance its own special kind of reality, while ordinary indicating feels merely empty and unreal.

Denouement   French for "unraveling"; that final portion of a story in which the loose ends are wrapped up.

Deputy   In an Equity company, a member of the cast elected to serve as the representative of the actors to the management. (See *Equity.*)

Downstage   At one time, stages were sloped to enhance the illusion of perspective, so when heading toward the audience, actors were literally moving "down" stage, and when backing away from the audience, actors were literally moving "up" stage. Even though our stages today are rarely sloped (or "raked"), we still use this terminology.

Dramatic   When the outcome of an event is important and cannot be foretold, we say it is *dramatic*. The essence is in wondering "What will happen?" (See also *Suspense.*)

Dramatic function   The job a character was created to do within the story. Can be related to plot, meaning, our understanding of the main character, or any combination of these.

Dress rehearsal   The final rehearsals that are conducted under performance conditions.

Dual consciousness   The actor's ability to be immersed in the character and the character's world, while still reserving a level of awareness for artistic judgment. Different types of material make different demands on actors; film requires the virtual elimination of the actor's awareness in favor of the character's.

Economy   Doing enough to fulfill the dramatic function and believability of the character but avoiding extraneous details or effort.

Emotion memory (or Recall) The actor's application of a memory from his or her real or imaginary past to enrich his or her response to the situation in the scene. While this device may be useful in rehearsal, it should never be used in performance for fear of taking the actor out of the here and now.

Empathy The actor's ability to put himself or herself in the place of another person, both for purposes of observation and for applying the Magic If to a role. It is possible to empathize with someone even if we do not sympathize with them.

Equity The Actors Equity Association (AEA), the main theatrical union for actors. *The Equity Rule Book* establishes the conditions under which actors may work in the theatre. Grievances are reported to the elected Equity deputy.

Exposition Providing information about what has happened before in order to help the audience understand what is going on in a story or scene. The difficulty in writing or playing exposition lies in not interrupting the action by falling into an "informational" tone. One old piece of advice is to "make exposition ammunition"; that is, your character must have a reason for providing expository information, and it must be justified by inner need.

Extra A nonspeaking actor who rounds out the reality of a scene. Professional extras in film are skilled workers who can repeat precise movements and blocking and know how to be believable without being distracting. Their union, the Screen Extras Guild (SEG), recently merged with the Screen Actors Guild (SAG).

Eye line In film, the direction in which you are looking must match the spatial relationship established by the camera in the scene. Usually the other actor will stand in a spot that will give you the correct eye line. When your eye line is "close to the lens" the other actor may be pressed up against the camera. The Director of Photography (DP) or the camera operator will guide you in providing the correct eye line.

Focus Whatever you are concentrating on at any given moment, usually your objective.

Functional traits Those traits that a character was given (or that you provide) to allow the character to believably fulfill his or her dramatic function in the story.

Givens More completely, the Given Circumstances; the world and situation within which your character lives, especially as they affect his or her action. The circumstances include who, when, where, and what.

Going up   Forgetting your lines. Although a terrible experience, forgetting your lines can sometimes provide wonderfully rich moments if you keep your action going, perhaps even resorting to paraphrase. Lines are learned more tenuously in film than on stage to guarantee the kind of freshness and authenticity the camera demands.

Head shot   The glossy 8 × 10 photograph an actor hands out along with his or her resume. The photograph should be attractive but not limiting in the way it portrays you—its function is merely to help someone remember you.

Improvisation   Performing without a script. While most comedic improvs are based on a scenario in which the actors have some idea of the basic beats of the scene and the climax, an "open-ended" improv may be based only on a situation or relationship. In traditional theatre, some directors use improvisation as a rehearsal device in which the actors explore their characters in situations beyond those contained in the script. Many good actors are terrible at improvisation, and many good improvisers are better at stand-up comedy than at characterizational acting.

Indicating   Showing instead of doing; that is, standing outside the reality of your character and playing the emotion or some quality of the character instead of immersing yourself in the experience of the action.

Indirect action   When some obstacle impedes direct action, a character may choose an indirect strategy, saying or doing one thing while really intending another. The obstacle may be internal or external. When there is indirect action, there is also subtext. (See also *Subtext*.)

Intention   (See *Objective*.)

Inner action   The inner process of reaction, attitude, need, and choice that results in outer or observable action. A believable performance integrates inner and outer action into one flow of stimulus and response. This integration is called *justifying* the external action by connecting it to an internal process.

Inner monologue   The "stream of consciousness" of the character. As a training or rehearsal device, actors sometimes verbalize or at least think through their characters' inner monologues to be sure they have provided full inner justification for their external actions.

Justifying   The process of connecting outer (visible or audible) actions to inner needs and processes. The script provides the basis for the outer actions; however much the script may also hint at the inner action which produces this outer action, it is ultimately the task of the actor to justify. In justifying, the actor puts his or her personal stamp on the performance.

LORT   The League of Resident Theatres; an organization that has negotiated a specific contract with Actors Equity governing the operation of regional theatres that maintain a resident company. Being a member of a resident company, including the various summer festivals, is the best growth experience an actor can have and is the traditional stepping stone from training to a professional career.

Magic If   Stanislavski's technique in which you put yourself in the given circumstances of your character *as if* you live in that world, then experience your character's needs *as if* they are your own, and finally choose and pursue your character's action *as if* it were your own. This process results in Metamorphosis or Transformation, whereby the actor "becomes" the character, though without losing the dual consciousness that provides artistic control. (See also *Transformation*.)

Matching   In film, the need to match details and emotional tone from shot to shot. (See also *Coverage*.)

Mark   In film and television, a piece of colored tape that shows the actor where to stand at a specific moment in a scene. The actor must "hit" each mark without looking down.

Master   (See *Coverage*.)

Metamorphosis (See *Transformation*.)

Moment   A brief period of time when something of special value is happening. We speak of "making the moment." Can also refer to one transaction between characters. Several moments make up a beat.

Motivation   The inner need that drives your character's action, which usually comes from something that has just happened in the scene, however much it may awaken some long-standing need in your character. It is important that the energy coming from this past motivation drives you toward some objective in the immediate future because you can't play motivation, only the action toward which it drives you. In other words, *motivation must lead to aspiration*.

Need   Whatever your character needs that drives him or her to pursue an action to try to satisfy that need. We sometimes distinguish between what we "want" and what we "need": The dancer *wants* to be able to move beautifully, but *needs* to work at the barre several hours a day to achieve this. Further, we don't always know what we need to get what we want. For the actor, however, either a want or a need will successfully drive action.

Objective   The goal your character pursues through action to satisfy a need. An objective is best defined using a transitive verb phrase, such as "to persuade him to give me a territory in town." In practice, the most useful form of objective is *a change in the other character,* such as "to get him to look at me with compassion." The terms *Intention* and *Task* are sometimes used to mean *Objective.*

Off book   Memorizing your lines so that you can perform without the script. During the period immediately after going off book, it is expected that you will need prompting (call for lines); call for lines without apology so that you do not lose concentration or your sense of action.

Out (or In)   On stage, away from center (or toward center).

Overlap   (See *Cueing.*)

Pace   The momentum or flow of a scene. Pace is different from tempo, which refers to the speed of the action. Regardless of tempo, a scene has good pace when the connections of cause and effect, action and reaction are strong and real so that the action flows with integrity and purpose. Paradoxically, sometimes slowing the tempo of a scene improves the pace because the actors are forced to experience the connections of action and reaction more fully.

Paraphrase   To use your own words in place of the words of the script, though with an effort to mean the same thing. Paraphrasing can sometimes help you to examine the meaning of your lines and to "own" or personalize them. It can also help carry you over moments in which you "go up" on your lines. In film and television, a modest amount of paraphrase is sometimes tolerated as a way of producing a more personal performance.

Personalization   The indispensable process of making the character's needs, choices, habits, and actions your own. (See *Magic If.*)

Playable   What we call an objective or action that is useful in performance and contributes to the movement of the scene. The most playable objectives are SIP: Singular, Immediate, and Personally important. The best way of defining an objective is as *a change in the other character,* as this will draw your energy outward and into the immediate future, bringing you into strong interaction with the other character.

Playing through Letting the action flow with good pace by keeping your awareness moving toward the future objective and avoiding falling into internal feelings or the past. *Your energy is most useful to the scene when it is oriented outward and toward the future.*

Plot The sequence of events as the story unfolds. The actor needs to be aware of how each of his or her actions moves the plot forward, and especially when a scene contains a *plot point* that must be solidly established.

Projection In the theatre, speaking loudly enough and with enough clarity to be heard and understood throughout the auditorium. Good projection is usually more a matter of clarity than of sheer volume. In film, however, any sense of projection will read as unreal. When Michael Redgrave, already an accomplished stage actor, did his first take for a camera, he asked the director how it was. The director, who was standing behind the camera, said, "It was fine, Michael, except I could hear you."

Prompt Book The copy of the script kept by the stage manager that contains the blocking, the lighting and sound cues, and all the rest of the physical aspects of a production. It is possible to recreate a production from the prompt book, as is sometimes done in the case of great European productions. Some of Shakespeare's plays were printed from his prompt books. In film, the script supervisor records every shot in a book, permitting the editor to access particular takes in a scene.

Prompting Giving actors lines when they ask for them. Actors usually call out, "Line." Lines are given by the stage manager in the theatre and by the script supervisor in film.

Prop Anything your character handles. In theatre, it is wise to begin working with rehearsal substitutes as soon as you are off book.

Public solitude Stanislavski's concept of how actors, by focusing on their objectives, can "forget" that they are in public and thereby avoid self-consciousness and stage fright. The concept does *not* imply that actors neglect the discipline of producing a publicly effective performance.

Read-through A rehearsal in which the entire scene or script is read aloud.

Reacting   Allowing yourself to respond to the immediate stimulus in the scene, and allowing that stimulus to make you do what your character does in response. This requires real hearing and seeing and the courage to surrender yourself to accepting the stimulus as your partner actually provides it, rather than playing what you have previously created in your head. Because everything your character does is in reaction to something, we say that "acting is reacting." The ideal is to be "more moved than moving."

Reel   A videotape containing a compilation of an actor's appearances on film. A reel may contain work in student films or classroom exercises. Although a reel may be useful in the early stages of a career, it is rarely worth the effort expended on making it.

Relationship   All characters exist in relationship to other characters, and we come to understand characters mostly by observing the way others relate to them. For this reason, we say that actors create each other's characters more than they create their own. It is important to develop your character in specific relationship to the performances of the other actors in your scene.

Relaxation   The key to most everything in acting. For the actor, relaxation is not a reduction of energy but rather a freeing of energy and a readiness to react. The term *restful alertness* is the best description.

Repertory   A company of actors that performs a body of plays. When a number of plays are performed on alternating days, it is called *rotating* or true repertory. The regional repertory movement in this country is an important source of entry-level jobs for young actors.

Resume   A listing of an actor's experience, showing the roles he or she has performed, including where and under whose direction, as well as training and special skills.

Running lines   Two or more actors going over their lines together. The best way to memorize lines.

SAG   The Screen Actors Guild, the main union for film and television shot on film. A powerful union with nearly 90,000 members, 94 percent of whom are unemployed at any given moment. An aspiring actor can join the union by being hired for a union job, though this is a catch-22. Some agents represent young actors informally even before they are members of the union, thereby giving them a chance to audition for union jobs.

Scene   A section of a play that has its own main conflict and crisis. A scene usually contains one of the major events of the story and makes a major change in the plot or central relationship. In a film or television script, scenes are also determined by changes in location or lighting requirements, and each scene is given a "slug line" as in INTERIOR LIVING ROOM—NIGHT. In some older plays, scenes are marked by the entrance of major characters; these are called *French scenes.*

Scenario A listing of the beats of a scene. Also called a breakdown, the scenario gives the actors a sense of the underlying structure of the scene; it serves as a sort of map as they move through the journey of the scene.

Score Stanislavski spoke of the score of a role as the sequence of objectives. The actor comes to understand the logic of this sequence and eventually this flow of action carries the actor through the role, serving as a kind of total choreography for mind and body. (See also *Spine.*)

Sense memory (or Recall) The use of a memory from the actor's real or imagined past of sensations similar to those required by a scene so as to enrich the actor's response to the scene. Stanislavski believed that every cell in the body is capable of such memory and urged actors to develop their storehouse of such memories.

Set up To prepare for the punch line of a joke, the entrance of a character, or some other important event. In television sitcoms, setting up a joke is called "laying pipe." In film, a set-up is one camera position.

Shot In film or television, one piece of film from one camera position, beginning when the director calls "action" and ending when he or she calls "cut."

Sides In the theatre, sides were small versions of a play that contained only the speeches of individual characters; these are rarely used now. In film, sides are miniature copies of the scenes to be shot on a given day and are distributed each morning by the second assistant director.

Spine Stanislavski spoke of each beat and scene in a role fitting together like the vertebrae in a spine. When the actor experiences this connectedness, the role begins to flow as if under its own power. Also called the *Through-line* of the role. Similar to the Score of the role, in which the through-line is understood as a sequence of objectives.

Spiritual action Stanislavski's term for the inner phase of action, which produces physical or external action.

Spontaneity   Each moment of a performance should feel as if it were happening for the first time and yet be controllable and consistent from performance to performance. Stanislavski believed that this can be achieved by an act being so fully rehearsed that it becomes "automatic and therefore free"; that is, because you don't need to think about it, you are free to experience it afresh each time you do it.

Stage fright   Everyone gets it. The only antidote is to be fully focused on the task at hand and passionately committed to it.

Stage directions   The indications in a script about the character's gestures, tone of voice, and so on, such as (*he moves away angrily*). Some teachers and directors tell actors to ignore stage directions because in some so-called acting versions of a play they may have been inserted not by the writer but from the prompt book of an earlier production. However, many writers provide stage directions, and you should consider them for the information they contain about the behavior and emotion of your character, even if that behavior eventually takes a different form in your particular production.

Stage right or left   Directions on a stage are given from the actor's point of view as he or she faces the audience; that is, stage right is audience left. In film, the director will say either "Move to your right," or "Move to camera left."

Stimulus   The thing your character is reacting to at any given moment. The most useful stimuli are in the immediate present, however much they may trigger needs or feelings from your character's past.

Strategy   Your character's sense of how best to pursue an objective within the given circumstances. The strategic choices the character makes express the way he or she sees the world and the other characters.

Subtext   When pursuing an objective indirectly, your character may be saying or doing one thing while really meaning another. For instance, if I want to tell you I love you, but am afraid you will reject me, I may approach the subject indirectly by talking about how stupid the people I work with are and how you are the only person who understands me. In such cases, there is a difference between the surface activity (the text) and the hidden agenda (the subtext). The character may be conscious or unconscious of the subtext; in either case, it is important that the actor avoid bringing the subtext to the surface of the scene by trying to play or indicate it. (This term is sometimes carelessly used merely to refer to the character's attitude about something or someone.)

Substitution A special kind of emotional recall in which someone from the actor's real or imaginary past is substituted (in the actor's mind) for the other character in a scene to enrich the actor's response to that character. This is a dangerous device because it may take the actor out of the here and now, but with caution it may be useful.

Superobjective The character's main desire in life; the life goal toward which each of his or her objectives is directed. Characters, like people in everyday life, are often unconscious of this life goal, but it pervades everything they do. Stanislavski also spoke of a superobjective *for the actor,* which is "to understand how every moment of the performance contributes to the reason why the play was written."

Suppression The choice *not* to act in response to a stimulus, but rather to "hold down" the energy the stimulus has aroused. By allowing yourself to feel the urge to act and then making the effort to suppress it, you can turn a "not doing" into a playable action. A "not doing" is useful because it helps build suspense.

Suspense A condition in which something is about to happen, but the outcome is delayed and in doubt. The more important the potential event, the more doubtful the outcome, and the longer it is delayed, the greater the suspense. The essence is the question, "What will happen?" which, from the actor's point of view, usually translates into "What will he or she do?"

Table Reading Usually the first rehearsal of a script in which the actors sit at a table and read it aloud. During any reading, it is important that the actors try to play in relationship and experience the action of the scene and not fall into a flat, "literary" tone.

Take In film, a single shot from "action" to "cut." There may be many takes of a given shot until the director is satisfied. The take intended for use will be indicated by the director saying, "Print it," though several takes may be printed to give the editor a choice of performances.

Task (See *Objective.*)

Technical Rehearsal   In theatre, the rehearsal in which the lighting, sound, and nearly completed set are first brought together under the command of the stage manager. At the technical rehearsal, the lighting and sound board operators have their first chance to rehearse their cues, and the designers are seeing the set and props in action. Great patience is required of the actors at a "tech" rehearsal, which is sometimes quite lengthy.

Tempo   The speed at which a scene is played; not to be confused with Pace. The actor must be able to justify the action at any tempo; Stanislavski would sometimes have actors play a scene at various tempos as a training exercise. Within a given tempo, there are variations which produce rhythm.

Temporhythm   The term used by Stanislavski to refer to the whole issue of overall tempo and the variations in tempo that produce the rhythms within a scene. He believed that the temporhythms of a scene are fundamental to the correctness of the action of the scene and "all by themselves" can move the actor to the correct emotion.

Through-line   (See *Spine*.)

Transaction   One give and take between the characters, sometimes also called a Moment. Each transaction can be judged by asking two questions: first, has one character truly affected the other? Second, does this "link" in the chain of action and reaction move the scene in the proper direction?

Transformation   The process by which the actor begins to "become" the character or, more accurately, make the character his or her "own." To use the language of William James, the character becomes a new "me" to be inhabited by the actor's "I." Stanislavski used the term *Metamorphosis*.

Universal   The quality of an action, event, or character trait that allows everyone to recognize and respond to it as related to their own lives.

Upstage   (See *Downstage*.)

Upstaging   In theatre, literally to position yourself upstage of the other character so he or she is forced to turn toward you (and away from the audience) to speak to you. In film or theatre, this term also refers to any behavior that draws attention to you and away from the other character. To be avoided at all cost.

Verb   The verb phrase that succinctly describes your action at a given moment, such as "to persuade." Only transitive verbs are used, and all forms of the verb "to be" (such as "being angry" or "being a victim") are avoided.

Visualization   The actor's ability to imagine a situation, to "see" it in the mind's eye. A special and effective form of rehearsal called Visuo-Motor Behavior Rehearsal (VMBR) allows you to visualize your performance while in a relaxed state, allowing your deep muscles to respond to your mental image.

INDEX

Note: Entries in this index do not duplicate listings in the Contents.